TURN YOUR MIND AND BRAIN BACK ON

Unleash the Power of a Renewed Mind

By

KIMBERLY DAVIDSON

Unless otherwise designated, all Scripture quotations are taken from the New International Version (NIV) and the New Living Translation (NLT).

Interior Design by Kimberly Davidson
Exterior Design by CreateSpace

ISBN-13:978-1724973276
ISBN-10:1724973274

Contents

Set Your Mind Free with Forgiveness

Put on the Mind of Christ

There is No Freedom without a Change of Mind

Don't copy the behavior and customs of this world, but let God transform you into a new person by changing the way you think. Then you will learn to know God's will for you, which is good and pleasing and perfect.

—Romans 12:2

1 — THE COMPLICATED MIND

This 34-year-old female started smoking and drinking at age14, and struggled with dieting and bulimia and binge drinking since she was 18-years-old. According to her, she went through men as fast as she rotated her wardrobe. Her resume was riddled with question marks— she'd been fired twice, laid off three times, and quit several jobs. Inside her head, whirled toxic thoughts of rejection, shame, bitterness, jealousy and depression.

Today this woman is happily married, alive; full of joy and purpose. Her obsessive-compulsiveness has diminished and she has thrown off the toxic emotions she carried as her identity. Jesus is the center of her life and her mind.

This woman is me, Kimberly Davidson. The day came when I knew my life was no longer working. In desperation, I cried to God, "Something's got to change. Please help me!" And He did. He released me from the act of bulimia. I call it a miracle; a recipient of undeserving grace and mercy.

Just like the disciples on the road to Emmaus, I didn't recognize it was Jesus. This miracle didn't change my mind—nor did I give up alcohol, men and my other vices. Not until I started studying the

Bible did I really come to know Jesus and recognize it was His power that set me free from this deadly disorder—not my self-will. Then I was in a place where He could begin the process of chiseling away and cleaning up my messed-up mind and life.

In 1902 James Allen wrote what is still considered a classic today, *As a Man Thinketh*. He stated that noble thoughts make noble people and negative thoughts make miserable ones. Most women have lived decades of their adult lives without exploring what their unconscious is trying to say through their thinking patterns and beliefs. Their childhood and adolescent memories of pain have been shoved away or minimized. They're depressed, addicted or living with stress-related illnesses. They're mad but don't express it. They've tried to be perfect and failed. Instead, they feel anxious and betrayed; miserable and taken for granted; used rather than loved. They feel guilty if they take time for themselves or ask for help.

Just like when we were in junior high school, our thinking is maligned with negativity. I have good news. *Your thought life doesn't have to control you. You can control your thought life.*

One beautiful day a man was walking along a California beach thinking that on the other side of the ocean was Hawaii. He asked, "Lord, would you build a bridge to Hawaii so I can drive over any time?"

The sky clouded over and a booming voice told the man, "Son, your request is very materialistic. Think of the logistics of that kind of undertaking. Take some time to think of another request that would honor and glorify me."

The man thought for a long time and finally asked, "Lord, I want to understand women's minds."

There was dead, darkening silence. Minutes later God answered, "My son, how many lanes do you want on that bridge?"

This silly old joke does emphasize a truism—women's minds are complicated. Take a moment and think about all the things you do every day that you're unaware of. There are thousands. Everything you do and every word you speak is generated by a single thought. Apparently, women speak about 25,000 words a day; a man speaks about 10,000. One man said, "My wife and I had words, but I didn't get to use mine." ☺

Experts believe humans process more than 50 experiences per second and have anywhere between 50,000 to 80,000 thoughts per day. That's an average of 2500 to 3500 thoughts per hour!

Research has shown that 33 to 50 % of all our waking thoughts are not focused on what we're doing or seeing in the moment, but are instead wandering around to other topics—which the mind finds more interesting than whatever we're doing in the moment.[1] You may actually be thinking right now, *Why didn't my boyfriend call? How much time will I have to study after this class ends? If my daughter is on her phone right now, she's grounded!*

Apparently, 98 % of our thoughts today are exactly the same thoughts from yesterday, and 80 % of them are negative—not only negative, but false and flat out wrong. William Hazlitt said, "Life is the art of being well-deceived." Did you know the inclination for self-delusion appears to be weaved into our genetic codes since the fall of mankind? We simply believe deep down that our judgment is better than the other guy's. We're totally unaware just how much we've been influenced by other people.

When a group of researchers evaluated decades of studies that measured how well people could distinguish truths from lies, they found that people's ability to spot deception was only a few percentage points better than a random coin flip.[2] Simply put, it's hard to tell when people are misleading you and when they're not. Remember the television program *The Newlywed Game*? We saw that getting to know someone often creates an illusion.

Growing up, we accept what we're taught without questioning. Every negative belief and self-talk message have been recorded in our brains and incorporated into our psyches. The left rational brain convinces us that our thoughts, beliefs and memories are true.

Jeremiah 17:9-10 states, *"The heart is deceitful above all things and beyond cure. Who can understand it? I the LORD search the heart and examine the mind …"* It's time to track to eradicate the lies and deceits with God's help!

RE-COLORING OUR LENSES

We see life through our own personal "colored lenses" which influences what we say and do today. It is our truth, our reality. Unless an outsider steps in, distortions in our belief system and faulty self-talk become ingrained and set us up to act in ways that guarantee the repetition of destructive patterns. And nothing will ever change until a force—God—enters our lives and frees our minds from untruths. Only He can enable us to see the world through His pure and true lens.

The reason our thought life is so important to God is that our thoughts are the *first* to be triggered in the chain reaction of our souls. Our *thoughts* stir up our *emotions* → stirs up *desires* → produces *actions*. If we can catch a negative thought before its first triggered, then we've got a good chance of being able to prevent some bad behaviors and sin from occurring in our lives.

Most of us have been ignorant to what the mind does and how it works—and to the fact that every Christian has been given the *"mind of Christ."* What does that mean? It means God's supernatural thoughts, or His holy Word, is accomplished in our lives by His supernatural power. Because of this ignorance, we haven't been able to use this incredible powerful gift God has given us. The Bible says, *"My people are destroyed from lack of knowledge"* (Hosea 4:6).

Lack of knowledge is the reason we believe untruths and get stuck. Knowledge is the investigation of the truth. Scientists say that our brains are wired to take in different streams of information from the eyes: One, for purposes of *understanding and knowing*, and two, for the purpose of *behaving accordingly*. The first stream—knowledge—is conscious, but the second stream—behavior—is more automatic and unconscious.[3] In other words: Knowledge → Behavior. *Knowledge of Jesus → Christlike behavior.* But here's the caveat—we must apply the knowledge and live it.

Proverbs 23:7 tells us that *a person is what she knows and thinks about all day.* Five verses later it says, *"**Apply** your heart to instruction and your ears to words of knowledge" (Proverbs 23:12).* If you understand something, you can begin to control it by choosing to make good life-giving decisions, rather than letting it control you. Throughout this study you will be working your brain and practicing mindful awareness—learning, observing, reflecting and responding.

The fact is: Without a change of mind, our lives will remain as they've always been, no matter what we do or what we try. No matter how many retreats we attend, how many books of the Bible we read, or how often we go to church, if we don't work with God on renewing our minds, we will still have the same problems and defeats.

See to It That No One Takes You Captive

Adolph Hitler's body guard in interviews was often asked whether he heard Hitler speak of the Third Reich's murder of 6 million Jews. He always replied no. In 2005 he said, "If Hitler really did all the terrible things people said he did, how could he have been our Fuhrer?" (Are you kidding me?) The evidence showed that under Hitler the Third Reich did horrendous things.

Paul wrote to the Colossian church, *"See to it that no one takes you captive through hollow and deceptive philosophy ..." (Colossians 2:8).* Why would Paul give us this advice? Because once we come to believe something is true we give it up grudgingly, or not at all. Once a belief takes root in our mind it becomes very difficult to dislodge it, hence the saying, "False beliefs die hard." To give them up threatens our sense of self.

We can choose to look for the truth or settle for untested perceptions. By settling for perceptions, we refuse to consider other possibilities. What if your thoughts aren't correct? What if they're not true? This is why we've got to examine them—those hollow and deceptive subjective philosophies—and remove them. This sounds impossible and it is. If we to ask God to reveal them to us, He will.

Throughout this book I reference brain science, called "neuroscience." To heal from painful experiences and consequently change our thinking patterns, it's very helpful to know what is going on at the biological (biochemical/brain) level. God has created our brains with the ability to recondition and rewire themselves on their own over time—*no matter our age!* We now know the brain is not as rigid as once believed but is pliable and changeable, called brain *plasticity* or *neuroplasticity* (*neuro* = brain cells; *plastic* = changed/altered).

This is good news and bad news. Our brains change with *everything* we experience—the good and the bad. This means the changes we make in our thoughts and behaviors can last as we create new brain structures and circuits. But it doesn't stop here. We don't just want to fill our minds with information, we want transformation.

"Transformation" means *a change in character.* God's goal isn't to fill the world with those who are merely truth-believers, but with people who shine with the brilliance of Christ, and live transparently before others, humbly showing them the way of Christ.

Brain expert Dr. Caroline Leaf wrote, "The moment people recognize the power of their minds—the individuality of their thinking and how they have control over their lives—then they are truly able to transform their world."

Here's the question you must answer: *Do I want to live a better story?*

† *How confident do you feel about your level of readiness for a radical mind and life change?*

1	2	3	4		5	6	7	8	9	10
Not confident										Extremely confident

2 — Nothing but the Truth, So Help Me, God!

A tale goes: A patient was told by his doctor he had a gigantic brain tumor and needed a brain transplant. The doctor said, "I have good news and bad news." Sadly, a couple was just killed in a car accident. The good news is you can have one of the brains transplanted. The man's brain costs $300,000; the woman's brain costs $60,000." Naturally he asked, "Why such a difference in cost?" The doctor replied, "The woman's brain is used." ☺

The human brain unbelievable; a symphony of complex systems that give life and sustain life. It probably won't surprise you to learn that the female brain responds more intensely to emotion. Feelings, especially sadness, trigger neurons in an area *eight times larger* in the female brain than in the male brain.[4] That explains a lot, doesn't it?

The encyclopedia states the "mind" collectively refers to the aspects of intellect and conscious processes manifested as combinations of thought, perception, memory, emotion, will and imagination.[5] The apostle Paul thought of the mind as something that has the ability to understand, to reason and to think; that a human's actions come from the inclinations of his or her mind (1 Cor. 14:14-19). Theologian Gregory "the Great" (AD 361) believed the image of God is found in our mind and soul.

Every experience we have weaves our feelings, thoughts, sensations and memory much like a tapestry. When woven together, both positive and negative events form connections in our brains. Science confirms that our negative self-talk gets stronger each time we repeat things such as "I'm worthless" or "I'm fat." Repetitively agreeing with any negative thought leads to anxiety and a state of deeper self-defeat. If this "stressed out" state continues for years, our brains don't function according to the "creation manual" and our bodies literally dysfunction.

Listen to this: Scientists have discovered that when we begin to contemplate something as complex and mysterious as God and the big questions in life, we have incredible bursts of activity firing up in different parts of the brain ... and we grow and heal. When prayer is added, many health benefits have been found, including greater length of life.[6]

It has been found that *12 minutes* of daily focused prayer over an 8-week period can change the brain to such an extent that it can be measured on a brain scan.[7] Toxic thoughts can cause brain damage—but *prayer can reverse that damage and cause the brain and body to thrive.*

Joseph Murphy wrote, "Little thought deposits made regularly over time compound to produce a large principal of mental abundance."[8]

Do You Want to Live a Better Story?

This was the question I asked you in the last section. How did you answer? Most of us do want to live a better story. There are a couple things we must do moving forward:

1. *Believe it's possible.* Jesus replied, *"What is impossible with man is possible with God" (Luke 18:27).*

2. *Do not be afraid of change.* God has an amazing plan for your life (Jeremiah 29:11).

3. *Start now.* John 9:4 states, *"We must quickly carry out the tasks assigned us by the one who sent us."*

4. *Don't give up!* You have a spiritual enemy, Satan, a.k.a. the devil, that will use whatever means possible to distract and disable you from moving forward. He does not want you to learn what God says in His Word or what is in this book. He is the master of sabotage, with a particular mission to get you off course with God, keeping you ignorant and blinded to the real freedom available in Christ. Recognize these as attacks and fight back. James 4:7 says, *"Submit yourselves, then, to God.*

Resist the devil, and he will flee from you." The key: Draw near and stay close to God.

"PUMP YOU UP"—OR NOT?

If you were a *Saturday Night Live* fan from the 1990's you no doubt remember, "Pumping it up with Hanz and Franz—the training program for the serious weight lifter." Most all of us, at one time or other, have attempted to "pump ourselves up," and not always with desired results. Listen to this diary entry:[9]

Dear Diary, I finally joined the local health club. I'm determined to drop 10 pounds and tone up. I want to look like I did 5-years ago. I made an appointment with a personal trainer named Antonio, a 26-year-old aerobics instructor and model for athletic clothing. I can't wait to begin!

MONDAY: *Tough to get out of bed at 5 A.M. but found it was well worth it when I arrived at the health club to find Antonio waiting for me. He is gorgeous and he promised to pump me up! He showed me the machines. I enjoyed his aerobics class immensely. He's very inspiring! He encouraged me as I did sit-ups, although my gut was already aching from holding it in the whole time he was around. This is going to be a fantastic experience!*

TUESDAY: *Wearily, I drank a whole pot of coffee, but I finally made it out the door. Antonio made me lie on my back and push a heavy iron bar into the air, then he put weights on it. Ugh! My legs were a little wobbly on the treadmill, but I made the full mile. His rewarding smile made it all worthwhile. I feel good!*

WEDNESDAY: *I dragged myself out of bed. The only way I could brush my teeth is by laying the toothbrush on the counter and moving my mouth back and forth over it. I think I have a hernia in both pectorals. Driving was okay as long as I didn't have to steer or stop. Antonio's voice is a little too perky for me this morning. He put me on the stair "monster." Why the heck would anyone invent a machine to simulate an activity rendered obsolete by elevators? I just tuned him out.*

THURSDAY: *The torture master was waiting for me. I couldn't help being a half hour late. It took me that long to tie my shoes. He told me to work out with dumbbells. I ran and hid in the restroom for rest of my hour.*

FRIDAY: *I cannot stand the sight of Antonio. If there was a part of my body I could move without unbearable pain, I'd hit him. He told me to work on my triceps. I don't have any triceps; they died! He sent me to the treadmill, which, as it got going faster and faster, flung me off. Humiliating!*

SATURDAY: *A day off—Yay!*

SUNDAY: *Church today; no gym—Yay! I considered dropping my membership until I got a glimpse of myself in the mirror coming out of the shower. Could it be? Is that a bicep? I think my hips look a little smaller? Are my eyes deceiving me? I tried on a pair of jeans I hadn't worn in quite a while and they fit perfectly! I can't wait to get back to the gym tomorrow!*

When the going gets tough, the tough get going—or do they? Erwin McMannus told an audience that people need permission to start; but people don't need permission to quit. *Resistance* is a powerful human reaction to challenging work. Statistics show that over 50 % of you will walk away from a study like this. Why? You've got good intentions *but* after spending your life building a way to handle life's tribulations, *your brain is hesitant to alter its underlying beliefs.* After all, even if your thinking and behavior is chaotic, it's helped you to survive. It's taken your brain decades to form beliefs and habits, and it's not easy to just change them.

To ready yourself to be freed from "empty deceptive philosophies," pray regularly and prepare yourself to inquire and investigate your thoughts. If you choose to go forward, once you begin this process, no doubt, you will experience what is called in psychology "cognitive dissonance." This is when a very strong conviction or belief we have is met with what our minds believe is contradictory evidence.

For example, God tells me that I'm awesome and wonderfully created (Psalm 139:14), but some kids at school have been calling me "ugly" since 4th grade. Therefore, telling me I'm awesome and beautiful will make me feel an *uncomfortable internal inconsistency*. To rid ourselves of the cognitive dissonance, our tendency is to take our belief and find evidence to support it.

Using this example, to support my belief that I'm ugly, all I have to do is look at some women's magazines. Then I'm 100 % convinced that the models are prettier than me. This automatically reinforces my belief that I'm ugly. Then those uncomfortable feelings (the cognitive dissonance) disappear because in my mind my false belief is confirmed, not God's truth.

This is exactly what the devil wants to happen! "I'm ugly and always will be ugly" is difficult to turn around because it's a deeply engrained belief, and my self-esteem and image are challenged. What we must recognize is *feelings are not facts*. We need to learn to question whether our emotions accurately reflect reality and truth. We need help; we need Jesus's supernatural intervention, who is described in the Bible as being *the* Truth (John 14:6).

Just like the determination we feel to transform our bodies through hard physical training, *making a commitment to change and work through this book with God can make a big difference in your life.*

Steve Maraboli said, "Let today be the day you love yourself enough to no longer just dream of a better life; let it be the day you act upon it." Pick up your pen and begin writing a better story! Pray Ephesians 3:20, "God, do for me what I can't do—the impossible."

Remember as you journey through this process you are a redemption story waiting to unfold. My goal through this book is to help you write a great ending to your story.

THE WORD OF GOD IS ALIVE AND POWERFUL

Quite often my house is filled with the smell of burnt food. Cooking is not my gift; just ask my husband! I open the windows, but the smell lingers. Eventually the fresh country air clears it away. It's the same with our toxic thoughts and feelings. We have to open the windows in our brains and let the clean, refreshing air of God's Word circulate through our minds.

God wants to transform our minds so we can start discerning truths from falsehoods which begins and ends with the Holy Bible. It is the ultimate validation of any truth. If you have a questionable or negative pre-conceived notion of the Bible and/or God, or you think it's only a book of ancient rituals, it deserves to be seen with new eyes. Think of the Bible as a manual for personal transformation that is an account of a community of human beings. God teaches us how to take care of ourselves and others. The overall message is that Love (God) creates, heals and renews; and frees His created from having to accept their "lot" in life.

The Bible is food, not burnt food, but truth food. It feeds the mind, heart, body and soul. As you ingest and digest God's Word, it dispels lies and becomes energy for life. Truth can be hard to understand because all human beings are limited in their understanding. This is why we need the Holy Spirit to guide us through the Scriptures into complete truth, and away from lies and deception in order to think, do and speak what is right and truthful (John 16:13).

The mind only has access to what it has learned. It can't use what it doesn't know. If only misinformation and lies is all you have access to, then your sunk. The solution: Begin learning and "downloading" God's Word into your mind. Hebrews 4:12 reads,

For the word of God is alive and powerful. It is sharper than the sharpest two-edged sword, cutting between soul and spirit, between joint and marrow. **It exposes our innermost thoughts and desires.**

This verse is telling us that the Bible penetrates deep within us and exposes our hearts and motivations. It is *active*, not passive. The words of this book are not merely stored in your brain as data in some file. They are words that enter your mind and heart with the power to transform your perceptions, emotions, decisions, principles, relationships and your will. These words find their way into your heart, giving wisdom, bringing courage and healing, whispering hope amidst the despair and sadness, and breaking each chain of bondage. Even if we don't completely understand something in the Bible, we trust and follow God. Scripture says,

- *"I am the LORD your God, who teaches you what is good for you and leads you along the paths you should follow"* (Isaiah 48:17).
- *"Do not merely listen to the word, and so deceive yourselves. Do what it says"* (James 1:22).

It's a fact: *Knowing and believing God's Word will change a person's life.* It will shift your self-identity. Before we can actually experience God's Word, we have to have faith. If we don't have faith in the author of the Word, then we won't experience much change. It's been said, "We tend to experience what *we expect* to experience."

For real mind renewal and transformation to occur, we need to experience who we are as defined by God. Let's pray, "Lord, help us to love Your Word and to study it and learn Your instructions for our lives, thereby transforming our minds and lives." Each time we open our Bible we ask the Holy Spirit to lead and teach us—to help us interpret correctly. As you pray and study each day ask,

- What does God mean by His words?
- What is God saying to me?
- What am I going to do about it?

3 — The Power of Strongholds— A.K.A. Mindholds

Let's do an attitude check. If someone had followed you around this past week, how would they describe you?

- Gracious or cranky?
- Complimentary or critical?
- Encouraging or bitter?
- Other?

Would it surprise you to know that scientists have proven that *75 to 98 % of physical and behavioral illnesses come from a negative thought life; only 13 % from diet, genetics and environment?*[10] There is a direct correlation between toxic thinking and illnesses such as cancer, diabetes, allergies, to name a few.[11] Simply put: Your body believes every word you say! Proverbs 14:30 says, *"A heart at peace gives life to the body, but envy rots the bones."* If we do not change our "stinking thinking" we can literally make ourselves sick. I know: In the past I've been diagnosed with lupus, gastritis, prediabetes and shingles.

What happens is: Thoughts associated with a painful or stressful experience release negative chemicals that travel through the body changing the shape of the receptors on cells lining our hearts; thereby increasing susceptibility to illness. Toxic experiences cause brain cells to shrivel and die, compared to positive experiences which make brain cells expand.[12] For example, we don't merely experience anger in our minds, we feel it biologically in our body—our muscles tense and stomachs ache. If we were to look at our brain, we may see a dark abscess caused by the stronghold of anger. The same is true for envy, anxiety, lust, fear, depression and other emotions.

When we experience a stressful feeling—anything from mild discomfort to intense sorrow, rage or despair—*there is a specific thought causing our reaction, whether we're conscious of it or not.* Toxic thoughts are generated from one of two seeds: the seed of *sin*, which is *voluntary* (we make a bad choice); or the seed of *woundedness*, which is *involuntary* (we had no choice). Since our brains are not wired for disorder, these lethal thoughts produce stressful feelings and toxic byproducts.

The good news is that *75 to 98 % of physical and behavioral healings come from a positive thought life.*[13] Healthy, truth-based thinking today has become an integral aspect of treatment for everything from allergies to liver transplants. When we think positively instead of negatively, our tolerance for pain is higher, our recovery from illness and surgery is quicker, and our blood pressure drops, our bodies release the good hormone DHEA *and* our brains release positive healthy chemicals. There's always hope!

MISCONSTRUED MESSAGES

You have an amazing brain! Did you know it stores every conclusion you make about every experience? And every new experience is treated as reality—until it's instructed to do otherwise. Every piece of information is stored with a certain importance attached to it (scientists call it an "image map").

It is the mind's job to believe whatever it has stored. This is why you believe you're right and others are wrong, and why you continually use misinformation in trying to process your feelings. (My objective in this book is to give you some tools and God's Word to help correct this.) Each image we collect in our brains is tagged with a feeling or feelings and is based on how we see and interpret the experience—called *perception.* Our personal values, judgments and learned responses are based on these experiences.

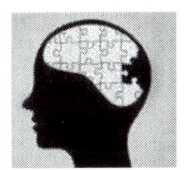 When we have a new experience, our brains automatically: Take a snapshot of what we see (*new experience*), then it finds the *old experience images* in our mind (like puzzle pieces) that *match our new present experience.* The closer the new experience connects to *an existing image,*

the more we will *see the new experience* in the same light. If the old existing image was displeasing, the new image will be displeasing. For example, Robyn's parents constantly fought "ugly" in front of her *(old image)*. Today when Robyn hears *anyone* raise their voice in conflict *(new image)*, she gets anxious and fearful.

We've trained ourselves to feel certain ways. Take for instance a documentary on a Stone Age Tribe. In one scene, they show the children and adults combing through the hair of the other tribe members, then picking out bugs and eating them. For that tribe, this is a tasty treat (and for my cats). Their collection of images tells them *Yummy!* For us—not so yummy. Our images tell us that hair bugs don't make a good meal.

When an experience has deeply wounded us, the images associated with that experience, along with the emotions we felt at that time—for example, hopelessness, rejection, worthlessness or not belonging—are forever attached to these images. This can create deadly thinking which takes over and structures our entire world. Joe called Ashley a "fat ugly pig," not once, but four times. His words hurt her badly. Even when Joe is in a good mood, when Ashley sees Joe walk into the room, or when she thinks of him, the feeling of anger comes over her.

What we need to recognize is our perspective on a particular situation may seem right and logical, but it will always be limited. God's perspective, however, is perfect. And as we continue to get to know Him through His Word we will begin replacing our error-based thinking and perspectives with truth. *Our image brain maps can change.*

† *Describe how do you think God wants you to move forward and grow.*

POWERFUL MINDHOLDS

Has anyone ever said to you something like, "You're so stupid" or "You'll never be able to do that." Or might you have thought to yourself, "I wish I were as pretty as her" or the dreaded "I should have … coz then I …" Perhaps you struggle with the shame of abuse or the anguish of battling depression. Over time, negative comments or feelings of inadequacy like these become "strongholds."

A "stronghold" is something that has a strong hold or powerful influence on a person. It is a mindset that is resistant to change. Synonyms are *stranglehold, vice-like iron grip, cancer* and *infection*. It's a deeply entrenched pattern of thought, behavior, philosophy or value, burnt into our minds through negative repetition. I call these mental strongholds or habits, *mindholds* because they are harmful thoughts and emotions which are literally embedded in our minds.

The most common strongholds are fear, pride, shame, envy, people-pleasing, low self-esteem, anger and unforgiveness, doubt, unbelief in God's character, perfectionism and bad habits. Negative beliefs are thoughtfully and emotionally wired into our minds with the intent to protect us from further pain, but unfortunately, they become a straightjacket.

Mindholds are also visible to the eye in a brain scan. Learning specialist, Dr. Caroline Leaf, author of *Who Switched Off My Brain?* states a stronghold literally looks like a cancer or abscess. For example, unforgiveness locks toxins in the body, which results in a heavy, dark memory. On the other hand, brain imaging illustrates that positive thoughts look like beautiful, lush and healthy green trees compared to negative thoughts which look like ugly, mangled, snarling thorn bushes. They upset the chemical feedback loops in your brain by putting your body in a harmful state.[14]

Toxic thoughts build toxic memories. Dr. Leaf asserts that if, for example, you have been repeatedly verbally or sexually abused as a child, all the thoughts associated with those experiences will release negative chemicals that travel through your body and can change the shape of the receptors on cells lining your heart, thereby increasing susceptibility to cardiovascular illness.

INVESTIGATE MY LIFE, O GOD

Remember what I said before: *75 to 98 % of physical and behavioral healings come from a positive thought life.* The question is: How do we cultivate a positive thought life? I say we courageously pray David's bold words in Psalm 139,

Investigate my life, O God, find out everything about me; Cross-examine and test me, get a clear picture of what I'm about; See for yourself whether I've done anything wrong—then guide me on the road to eternal life (23-24, MSG).

Many of us are scared to death to pray this for fear of what God will reveal. Not to worry! God is like a gentle surgeon, carefully revealing and then excising the toxicity that plagues us. I'm reminded of an old rabbinic parable (similar to Jesus's parable in Luke 8:4-11 about the seed that fell on the rock, the path, the thorns and the good soil). It goes:

These are the four types of students that sit in the presence of the rabbis: the sponge, the funnel, the strainer and the sieve. The sponge soaks everything up. The funnel takes it in and lets it out the other side. The strainer lets it out and retains the sediment. The sieve removes the sediment and retains the fine material.

Which do you think is the best student? It's the sieve, who sifts through what its being presented and retains only the best. Toxic thoughts must be identified and interrogated—the unhealthy sediment must be removed and replaced with the fine material of God's Word. Then our brains and minds change which means our lives change!

† *What daily and weekly pattern can you commit to that will likely help you spend time with the "fine material of God's Word"?*

4 – THE POWER OF THE MIND

What female hasn't fallen into the diet trap! My life revolved around dieting, first becoming an obsession, then a deadly eating disorder for 16-years. I *believed* my weight was equated to my significance. Each day I'd begin a new diet. Inevitably I'd be tempted to eat something loaded with fat or sugar, like *Fritos* and almond cookies—my favorite comfort foods!

Then my mind would go down this path of all-or-nothing thinking, "You blew your diet! You might as well just pig out and start all over again tomorrow." So I did. Then I'd feel fat and miserable. So, I'd throw the food up and feel worse.

Inevitably I'd compare myself to someone who I admired—a woman who was skinny and popular and successful. I'd say to myself, "I know she's not sitting at home by herself pigging out. She's got a real life. The kind of life I want!"

Toxic self-talk alleged, "Kimberly, you're bad, weak, a loser." Then positive self-talk would reply, "Tomorrow I'll be good and strong and stick to my diet—then I'll be a winner!" It didn't happen because the toxic talk always won the battle.

"Just stop" or "Go away thought" doesn't work. Behavior modification doesn't cut it. Only when we allow God to cleanse out the garbage that's been programmed into our minds will wrong actions be corrected and eliminated—hence the phrase *garbage in— garbage out*.

THE FOUR STEPS

We all want to know how to get in sync with God and transform our minds. God will do His part *if* we're willing to do our parts. The process can be broken down into four steps:

1. *Create a new habit of worship*—of connecting with God.
2. *Take biblical action*—follow God's instructions.
3. *Believe*—you have the mind of Christ.
4. *Take up your new position*—in your new self.

Before we talk about these specific steps, there are some things about how our minds work that we should understand.

THE POWER OF THE UNCONSCIOUS MIND

Jesus said, *"This is why I speak to them in parables: Though seeing, they do not see; though hearing, they do not hear or understand."* (Matthew 13:13). Jesus knew forces outside of our conscious awareness operate in our minds—often preventing us from seeing and dealing with things that are right in front of us. An understanding of how our minds operate unconsciously can keep us from becoming one of those who do not see or hear.

We have a single unified mind that operates in both conscious and unconscious modes. There is a constant interplay between these two parts of our brains, and with what is going on in the world outside us, and what is happening inside our heads.

The *unconscious mind* is the part responsible for all of our involuntary actions and describes how our minds filter what we are experiencing. We don't have easy access to the information stored in the unconscious. The *conscious mind* only works when we're awake and makes us aware of the present moment. Whereas, the unconscious works 24 hours a day. It makes up 90 to 95 % of who we are; compared to our conscious which makes up 5 to 10 % of who we are. When we're sleeping our unconscious is busily working on our important goals.

E. Stanley Jones states it well, "The conscious mind determines the actions—*present day behavior*—the unconscious mind determines the reactions—*based on past experiences*—and the reactions are just as important as the actions."

Tanya's husband Colton believed in corporal punishment and frequently spanked their children with his belt. This is because his father did the same thing. Colton developed an unconscious belief about a father's authority: *for a man to be respected in his home, he must be feared by all who live there.* He learned this from his father which made him believe that if he didn't dominate the members of his family, then he'd be a failure as a man and a father. If he desires to transform his thinking, he needs to become aware of his unconscious beliefs. Colton did begin to see that his beliefs from his past caused him to act this way. Then things began to change in his home.

During childhood, we acquired countless memories and experiences that formed who we are today. However, we cannot recall most of those memories. But, they are unconscious forces, beliefs and personal experiences, that drive our behaviors today— they bleed into the present. The *unconscious* decides where and how your memories are stored. It may hide certain memories, such as traumas, that have strong negative emotions until you are mature enough to process them consciously. When it senses you are ready, whether you consciously think you are or not, it will bring them up so you can deal with them.

The unconscious is our mind's way of keeping us from thinking and feeling everything at once. That would be overwhelming. Since God didn't design us to deal with everything all at once, we can't be fully aware of *all* that is going on inside our minds at any given point in time. That may lead you to ask: *Do I have free will?*

DO WE HAVE FREE WILL?

Brea (her name has been changed) came to our women's' Bible study every week. She soaked up God's Word, asked a lot of questions and raved how good our teacher was. Yet, whenever stress occurred in a relationship (usually with her husband), Brea became a different woman. She'd "gaslight" the people who were trying to help her, eventually driving them away. (*Gaslighting* is an emotional manipulation tactic in which a person in order to gain more power, twists the truth to make a person question their reality.)

It's natural to think, "Well, I guess Brea really isn't a Christian." Do you know someone who has this kind of Dr. Jekyll, Mr. Hyde personality? Sweet and kind one moment; then on a rampage the next. Scientists have revealed that early chronic stress/early child adversity reprograms how we will react to stressful events for our entire lives. For these people, they can react to something we'd consider miniscule as if it is a matter of life or death. They trigger easily, hyperreactive to very small stressors. They may also have what's called *Borderline Personality Disorder.*

The mind can only use the material it's aware of. Deep influences from our past ("past" is anything that occurred before this moment) have been shown to influence our behavior today. Life lingers and we carry experiences over from one situation to the next without realizing it. If we've had a chaotic or difficult childhood, today we may have difficulties in intimate relationship. Yet it rarely occurs to us that the problem resides in the hidden files of our personal history.

Events in our environment can often automatically trigger a not so nice behavioral response. *Without realizing it, we keep repeating the past in an attempt to get it right.* Rather, our focus is on the conscious present because that's the part of our mind that's trying to understand what's going on. We're unaware there's *a great deal* whirling around in the unconscious.

Let me add as a second response: If our knowledge of God and the Bible remains immaterial and we stick with our own perceptions (hidden files), we won't be able to adequately deprogram our brains of misbeliefs. *For real mind renewal and transformation to occur, we need to experience who we are as defined by God.* We must *experience* what He says about us concretely and vividly.

FREEDOM FROM "HIDDEN FAULTS"

Legendary Cleveland Indians pitcher Bob Feller, speaking of his fast ball said, "You can't hit what you can't see."

How do we control so many unconscious influences? The great king David, who the Bible described as a man after God's heart, had an honest moment with God. He wrote,

How can I ever know what sins are lurking in my heart? Cleanse me from these hidden faults. And keep me from deliberate wrongs; help me to stop doing them. Only then can I be free of guilt and innocent of some great crime (Psalm 19:12-13).

David is imploring God to show him and cleanse him from any *hidden faults*. The Amplified Bible calls these faults "hidden and unconscious." These things we have tucked away in our unconscious or simply shoved away so we don't have to deal with them. God is the One who can show us what they are then free us from the toxic thoughts and emotions we carry.

If we deny our "hidden faults" and don't allow Him to expose and deal with the root causes of our issues—because we deny their existence and only concern ourselves with the symptoms—then those symptoms keep returning and the unconscious thoughts hijack behavior. We end up discouraged, depressed and convinced God doesn't care about us. And Satan rejoices.

Some people who have been traumatized often *compartmentalize*. Certain memories are kept hidden—vaulted off—from the conscious self. What is hidden may leak into the conscious awareness through nightmares, flashbacks or intense emotions that have become separated from the memory of the incident. The traumatized, particularly abuse survivors, can't—or won't—access certain parts of themselves. They try to seal off the pain. It's not a conscious choice.

In my case, my conscious chose to binge and purge (bulimia), yet the act was driven by my unconscious's need for emotional pain relief. Any coping mechanism mentally transforms a situation into something different and easier to handle.

Unless we learn to become aware of the beliefs we hold in our unconscious, we will continue to battle with ourselves and never win. This is a picture of lack of free will. For mind transformation to occur, we can take advantage of the power of both the unconscious and conscious and change how we feel and what we do. Then we exercise our free will.

† *Acknowledge you have hidden influences. Tell God you want to do something about them. Ask God to release from your unconscious the first issue He wants to work on with you.*

THE POWER OF BELIEF

The mind is powerful—but also easy to manipulate and deceive. That is what the advertising industry banks on … and why Satan targets our minds. No doubt you've heard of the *placebo effect*. It is a counterfeit treatment which produces powerful positive results in the body's chemistry due to the effect of suggestion. It highlights the strong relationship between mind and body. It has an evil twin called the *nocebo effect* which refers to the power of *negative* suggestion that can lead to bad health, toxic thinking, even 'death by hypochondria.'

The children's story "The Little Engine that Could" is all about the power of belief. This secular culture claims there is no greater power than belief in the power *of self* and the ability to manifest all *self's desires*. There is incredible power in what the self (ego) believes, which is why self-help books consistently sell.

This is what I've learned about the power of the mind and belief and God. I teach a Christ-based abuse recovery class at a women's prison in their treatment center for recovering addicts. In each class I'd say only 10 % of the ladies are authentic Christ-followers. The other 90 % avow that God is their "higher power." The majority of the women in this program graduate and are highly committed to stay clean and begin a new life. This made me wonder about people who choose higher powers other than Christ and succeed staying sober in programs like AA (my brother is one example).

The Alcohol Research Group in California found that alcoholics that believed in God as their higher power were most likely to make it through the stressful periods of life with their sobriety intact. As Christians we say, "Of course!" But it wasn't God that mattered, the researchers figured out. It was their *belief* in a God of greater power. God was their placebo. The precise mechanism of people's beliefs are still little understood. But we do know for lifestyle habits to permanently change, people must first *believe* change is feasible.

JESUS IS NO PLACEBO

The mind is God's creation. Belief is God's idea. But as Christians we can be *assured* of permanent internal transformation when we believe in the saving faith of His Son Jesus Christ. Jesus came down to earth as the living embodiment of God Almighty. He didn't merely tell but showed us humans what humans created in God's image could become. When He returned to the Father in heaven, Jesus sent the Holy Spirit and His unbridled power was released into all believers. Deuteronomy 8:18 states, *"But you shall remember the LORD your God, for it is He who is giving you power to …"* That power transforms our belief into the miraculous.

Jesus said, *"… you are in me, and I am in you" (John 14:20)*. God unites us to Himself (John 17:21). A new dynamic happens—we get God's spiritual DNA (so to speak) and we come to life. God's nature, His spiritual DNA, living in me, gives me the desire and the ability to create a whole new life, to think and act more like Jesus—and is the foundation for victory!

By bringing you back to Himself through the work of Jesus Christ, God has established relationship with you. Now He is committed to your transformation … but you have to do your part. Simply put: Belief in Jesus Christ is not a placebo. Belief in Him is the *real* deal.

The Power of Habit

What did you do first thing this morning? How did you get your kids off to school? What did you eat for lunch? When you got home from work, what did you do?

I think we can all agree that our lives are a mass of habits, many of which we do unconsciously and automatically. We may think we're acting on a well-considered decision, but we're not. Researchers believe anywhere between 40 to 90 % of what we do every day isn't executed by actual thinking decisions, but habits.[15] [16]

Repetition is the engine that strengthens and perpetuates what has captured our desire. Repeated experiences become first a habit, then an addiction, becoming *robust networks* in the brain, becoming more efficient with repetition. So, the habit gets deeper.

The thing about habits is they're encoded into brain structures—called "habit loops" stored in the *basal ganglia* of the brain. This is an advantage because it would be awful if we had to relearn how to drive after each trip to the store. If you had a brain injury to the basal ganglia, you'd lose access to hundreds of habits you rely on every day.

The problem is the brain can't differentiate between a good or bad habit. Deadly habits are difficult to unlearn and break. A habit, once strongly established, creates a brain map that reinforces itself and prevents other habits from being formed.[17] So, if we have a bad habit, it's always lurking in the brain waiting for the right cues and rewards to express itself. This explains why it's so hard to create a new habit or change an old one. We're not aware that our habit loops are always growing, and we're blind to the ability to control them.

Over time, our habits shape who we are. As we nurture them, we choose to bend our will until we no longer choose a different route, becoming a slave to that habit. Like a slave, we submit ourselves to its wicked demands. If it is pleasurable enough it is more likely to be repeated more often which can lead to an addiction. It may even end up destroying us.

Going against a well-entrenched habit will be a challenge, but not impossible. The good news is if we choose to create a new pattern/routine, the new pattern becomes as automatic as any other habit—assuming it's a good habit. On the other hand, if we choose a bad pattern it could be a curse.[18] The choice is ours.

† *How confident do you feel about your level of readiness to create a brand-new habit and go against some well-entrenched habits?*

1	2	3	4		5	6	7	8	9	10
Not confident										Extremely confident

5 — DEADLY DECEPTION AND ACCUSATION

In the classic story *Pinocchio*, Geppetto the woodworker creates a boy out of wood. He wishes he would become a real boy. His wish is granted and Pinocchio is transformed into a human boy with a mind of his own. His boyish ideas land him in with the wrong crowd and he runs away from home, which breaks his father's heart (reminds me of the "Prodigal Son" parable in Luke 15). When each one of us is left with "a mind of our own" chaos, hurt and rumination can quickly ensue.

How do you feel when someone criticizes you with (what you perceive to be) harsh words, sarcasm, ridicule or judgments? It's horrible. It may even be nonverbal; when someone gives you a look of disgust, disdain, even hatred. These actions are often at the root of "rumination." *Ruminate* means we reflect on something *repeatedly* in our minds; we over-analyze; worry about a past stressful event; we wrestle with the future.

We weren't born having negative thoughts about ourselves and other people. These evolved as we encountered people and situations that fed us deceptive and accusing messages and beliefs. Unaware, we swallowed these powerful toxins each day. Scientists say positive emotions are fewer in number than negative emotions. Generally, we have a ratio of 3 to 4 negative emotions to one positive emotion.[19] Dr. Clifford Nass at Stanford University explains,

> The brain handles positive and negative information in different hemispheres. Negative emotions generally involve more thinking, and the information is processed more thoroughly than positive ones. Thus, we tend to ruminate more about unpleasant events.[20]

Anxious people have a harder time suppressing negative thoughts and get caught up in the repetitive practice of rumination[21]—of chewing on a thought or a situation, just like a dog chews on a bone, always connecting the thought back to some perceived unchangeable and negative aspect. It's a recipe for depression and the blues.

This is because criticism lingers. According to Chad Hall, Director of Coaching at Western Seminary, hearing criticism is not only painful in the moment, but it piles up and continues to do harm by keeping us in a stressful state.[22] Every criticism stored in our minds is our "reality"—our measure of truth. Just as the pain from one criticism begins to heal, a critical person opens the wound back up by firing another painful dart. Each new remark goes right onto the previous pile.

It's a fact: We carry around words of criticism for far longer than we do words of affirmation or encouragement. This is because our *personhood, our soul*, is attacked; compared with "feedback," which addresses our *behavior*. We carry around what I call "soul dirt."

The tracks grow deeper and stronger every time we believe that another person has confirmed a particularly strong toxic thought; *That was really dumb of me*. We then feel even more *deficient, rejected, defeated, alienated, bad, unlovable, unacceptable.*

For example, Sara's mom constantly tells her she isn't good enough. When her teacher tells her that her homework assignment didn't meet class standards, Sara repeats to herself *again* that she is not good enough, making that toxic thought track deeper and harder to get out of.

Critical words have a long life and remain toxic long after we think we've disposed of them. They create wounds that destroy beliefs and ideas of logic, order, goodness and God. If we were better judges of reality we'd be able to reject the harmful words. This is why we need God's Word, and honest and safe people in our lives—to speak truth and reality. Otherwise, we keep picking up those deceptive and accusing remarks and ruminate on them unceasingly. Answer:

- *True or false:* When I run into something troubling, my thinking runs through all kinds of scenarios.
- "I tend to ruminate on something that bothers me [*75% or 50% or 25% or ___%*] of the day.

THINGS MIGHT HAVE BEEN DIFFERENT ...

Are you one of the many women who've had a stressful and/or chaotic life and consequently ruminate about how you'd have liked things to be different? *If only; I should have; I could have; Never; I can't.* Other words are: *"would," "ought"* and *"I wish I; I wish you had ..."* Do these sound familiar: *It used to be... It could have been.*

Valerie's son became ill and she took him to the doctor, who diagnosed him with an ear infection. He got worse. Valerie took him to the Emergency Room. The doctor shared the same diagnosis. However, her son only got worse. She took him back to the ER where they diagnosed him with meningitis. Because his condition was so advanced, he died that day. Riddled with guilt, for months Valerie ruminated, *"If only I ..."* She judged herself as failing her child and began drinking to diminish the pain.

The truth was that she had no medical training. She took her son each time to physicians, who missed the diagnosis. She had fallen into the trap of judging herself on the outcome—rather than on her good actions and intentions.

When we feel we've lost control, it's easy to ruminate. All ruminating is good for is muddling our brain circuitry, re-wounding ourselves, stressing us out, leading to feelings of guilt, condemnation, depression and other mental and physical disorders. These strongholds take us captive if we continue to feed and give power to the thoughts.

If you want to get your thinking on track with the mind of Christ, learn to ask yourself this very important question, *"How can it be helpful and healthy to argue with or ruminate on something which has already happened or has not happened?"* Answer: It's not helpful.

POPULAR TOXIC PHRASES

Take the word *should*. How many times a day do you say or think, "I should …" or "My husband/boyfriend should …" or "That person should …" or "This organization should …" When we create "should-thoughts," we are wanting reality to be different than it is. Let me also add, if you beat yourself up with a lot of *"I should have …"* statements, *please* tell yourself, "I was doing the best I could at the time." Pay attention to how many times a day you say "should."

These two phrases are popular: *"You need to …"* or *"I want you to …"* Much of our anxiety comes from living outside of our own business. When I start ruminating on the *"You need to …"* or *"I want you to …"* I'm in your business and I need to get out. Your business is between you and God. When I'm in your business, then I'm not in my own and I wonder why my life isn't working so well (a technique called *deflection)*. I think there's only one exception: if you're a parent and are teaching your child responsibility.

Peter said to Jesus, *"Lord, and what about this man?" Jesus said to him, "... What's that to you? You follow Me!" (John 21:21-22).*

Ask, "Whose business is it?" If it's not yours, then you have no reason to feel anxious. Simply put, to think that I know better than God what's best for someone else is arrogance. And it only results in muddled brain circuitry.

We need to get this: *Much of the stress we feel is usually caused by arguing with something that is NOT reality!* We're either living in the past or future tense. Things in the past tense can't be changed; it's history and unalterable.

We've got to focus on where we are—not where we wanted to be, or thought we should be, or wishing something hadn't been. I'm sorry, but that's not reality. The present is today. Today counts. We can't change the past nor control the future. *We need to accept "what is," fix our eyes on God and leave the results to Him.*

Mind transformation starts with thinking: *This way of living and thinking is no longer an option,* and praying Psalm 25:5, *"Guide me in your truth and teach me."*

✝ *In what ways do you tend to get into other people's business? Can you explain your motives? Give a specific example.*

ATES AND PMSS (A.K.A. THINKING ERRORS)

Byron Katie wrote in her book *Loving What Is,* "Behind every uncomfortable feeling, there's a thought that isn't true for us."

Like generations of women who've gone before me, I too made the same mistake of taking on what God did not gift or intend for me to take on. When the church I attended found out I was a seminary student, they said, "We have a job for you! We want you to direct women's ministries."

Instead of standing up for myself and telling the board that leading this ministry was not what I believed God called me to do *and* taking this to God in prayer to seek His will, my need to please and achieve something important kicked in. So, I accepted. To back out would have been far worse. For 3-years I was frustrated and bitter. I felt guilty for feeling that way. At one point my leg broke out with shingles. (We know chronic stress leads to unregulated inflammation which translates into symptoms and disease.) I habitually thought, *If I don't put on a happy face, Jesus and the church leaders will be disappointed in me.* Lie! This thought wasn't true for me.

It is amazing how deceptive other people can be. But the number one person who gets away with deceiving us is ourselves. We can choose to look for the truth or settle for untested perceptions. By settling for unproven perceptions, we refuse to consider other possibilities. Have you ever asked yourself: *What if my thoughts aren't correct? What if they're not true?* Thoughts are not events. They are not objective (means something most people agree upon)—they are *subjective* (means perceived reality; *I think; therefore, it is*). It's our subjective thoughts that run our lives—and they may be incorrect.

A huge number of women live by "Automatic Thinking Errors" (ATE) and have fatal PMS of the mind: "Powerful Mental Strongholds." We create them because we don't want to be blindsided by hurt or caught off-guard. They're often a defense against shame. ATEs and PMSs can become *idols* when we look to them to run our future. Romans 6:1 asks a rhetorical question: *Don't you realize that you become the slave of whatever you choose to obey?*

Like a computer virus, it's not always easy to detect an ATE and PMS in our belief system because they're so engrained and have become habitual and automatic. We don't realize we have them. Unfortunately, they completely block our ability to clearly think things through and live as God desires. The good news is God designed us to constantly change. We don't have to do what our ATE | PMS says! Pastor Sam Adeyemi wrote in his book *Success is Who You Are,*

Thoughts are powerful. They can totally revolutionize your life. There is no force in this world that is strong enough to hold you down when you change your thoughts to fit God's plan for your life.

"Your mission, should you choose to accept it," is to become aware of, and then, quickly capture your deceptive thoughts, investigate, and then, reframe them with truth. Socrates said the unexamined life is not worth living.

✝ *Why might you be afraid to allow your thinking to be changed? For example, fear of the unknown?*

CAPTURING THE MOST COMMON ATEs & PMSs

Choosing what voice we listen to matters—a lot! The truth is: There's a part of us that doesn't want to let go of our favorite ATE|PMS because it's familiar and comfortable; even an idol. We think we're doing just fine. We don't realize we're saying, *"I'd rather not run the risk of being empowered and free. I won't let the pain go."*

To help yourself dig up the wrong voices and false beliefs, go through this list of the most common ATEs and PMSs. There are suggested investigative questions to help you uncover truth, thereby, changing your reality. Ask a friend, family member, or counselor to help you.

All-or-Nothing Thinking ("black and white" thinking). This person thinks automatically in absolute terms, like "always" or "every" or "never." "I *always* mess this up. I'll *never* be a success." "You can *never* be trusted."

Ask yourself and God: "Am I looking at the negatives, while ignoring the positives? Is there a more balanced way to look at this situation?"

People Pleaser (fear of man): This person thinks, "I must be loved or approved by every significant person in my life. I depend on others for my value."

Ask yourself and God: "Who am I doing this for—me, others, God? Am I trying to manufacture feelings of safety?"

Exaggerates/Overgeneralization. This person automatically makes wide amplifications or generalizations (often to avoid taking responsibility or to deflect blame). For example, she sees a single negative event, like not getting a promotion, as a never-ending pattern of defeat.

Ask yourself and God: Put the situation in perspective. "What are the good things about the situation? What can I do to change it and see it the way God sees it?"

Evasive/Deflects/Vague. An "evasive" person uses the phrase "I don't know" to avoid difficult, stressful or embarrassing questions and issues. "Deflecting" is automatically changing the subject or shifting the focus off yourself and onto someone or something else. "Vagueness" is avoiding concrete, truthful answers to questions.

Ask yourself and God: "Why don't I want to talk about the details of my life? What fears are keeping me defeated? What are the facts and truth, versus my own interpretations?"

"I Can't … Yes, but." These words are indirect forms of resistance and the word "no." Some say this to express their refusal to take responsibility and accountability, which is really saying, "I don't want to" or "I won't." Others say it due to low self-esteem. Someone important may have told her she could never do anything worthwhile. To say "I can't" is to say we don't believe God's Word which says, *"I can do all this through him who gives me strength"* *(Phil. 4:13).*

Ask yourself and God: "Am I saying this because I don't want to; or because I don't believe I have the ability to actually do it; or because I don't want to rely on God?"

Mind-reader. This person jumps to conclusions and assumes the intentions of others. She is convinced that her prediction is a fact, therefore, will have set consequences.

Ask yourself and God: "What's the evidence to prove this will turn out this way? How do I know what other people are thinking? Just because I assume something, does that mean I'm right?"

Catastrophizes/Worries (Life-or-Death). This person is consumed by fear and automatically assumes something negative is going to happen when there's no evidence to support it. Psalm 37:8 says, *"Fretting only causes harm and leads to evil."* (Worry turns into anxiety, which turns into depression, which is trauma to the brain.[23])

Ask yourself and God: "What are the truth-based facts? How do they counter my interpretation? Am I going ahead of God which shows lack of trust in Him?"

Personalizes. This person holds herself personally responsible for an event that is out of her control, like Valerie did when her son died.

Ask yourself and God: "Am I really to blame and why? Am I making this all about me? What other explanations might there be?"

Victim/Blames. A victim unconsciously thinks, "My past strongly affected my life and continues to do so (blame). I can't help the way I am." The good experiences don't count because in her mind only bad things happen to her, which is usually someone else's fault. She may also feel she's always wronged, the opposite of accountability.

Ask yourself and God: "What's the best that can happen in this situation? How can I amend it? Why don't I believe this truth: *"You, dear child, are from God and have overcome them, because the one who is in you is greater than the one who is in the world" (1 John 4:4)?"*

Jealous/Envious. This person compares and covets what someone else has: material things, a person (like a friend's boyfriend), or physical traits. Making one-sided comparisons leaves her feeling inadequate; or she does it to make herself come out on top (pride).

Ask yourself and God: "Why am I comparing myself with someone who is created totally different than me, with a different purpose? Am I making fair comparisons? Am I trying to create feelings of safety?"

Prideful. This person seeks to satisfy an inner longing for value and esteem. Pride is a sin from which other sins arise, such as selfishness, judgment, insensitivity, self-justification and vanity.

Ask yourself and God: "What do I fear by having my prideful nature exposed *and* removed? Do I want to live on self-will or submitted to and powered by God?"

Judgmental/Critical. This person finds fault with everyone else. She labels people. To feel good about herself, she demonizes other people, particularly those who have wounded her. Jesus said, *"Do not judge, or you too will be judged" (Matthew 7:1).* Wayne Dyer wrote, "When you judge another, you don't define them, you define yourself."

Ask yourself and God: "What am I saying about myself?"

"Need-love." This person is relationally dependent. When she says, "I love you," she's really saying, "I need you. I want you to take something of yourself and fill the emptiness inside me with it." The opposite is *agape love:* an "unselfish, thoughtful, unconditional, sacrificial love which doesn't expect anything in return." God agape loves us and agape love is how God created us to love others.

Ask yourself and God: "Is my agenda to enhance and give (as in a gift) to my beloved, or solely to fill myself?"

"Downward Social Comparison." This person mentally transforms setbacks to make them seem lesser in order to cope emotionally and/or evade accountability. She reminds herself there's always someone worse off; her adverse experiences weren't near as bad as

compared to others. She thanks God she's not in their shoes and is convinced she's over her troubles.

Ask yourself and God: "Is my agenda to really thank You for my blessings, or solely to evade the discontentment in my life?"

† *Describe how your ATE|PMS helps meet your needs. For example, "My pride meets my need for love and affection."*

True Mind Transformation

Then you will know the truth, and the truth will set you free.

–John 8:32

6 — STEP ONE: CREATE A HABIT OF WORSHIP

No doubt you're familiar with *Pepsodent* toothpaste. Back in the 1950s Claude Hopkins turned Pepsodent into one of the best-known products on earth. He helped create a toothbrushing habit which spread like wildfire across America. The secret to his success is he found a *cue* and *reward system* that fueled this tooth brushing habit. His discovery was so powerful that today video game designers, food and cosmetic companies and hospitals use the same principles. Hopkins created a craving in his customers.

To turn on the mind of Christ, likewise, we need to create a craving for Jesus (powering the habit loop)—create *a desire*. As my dear friend says, "*I want* the fire of God to burn in me." Then we pursue our desire:

- Create a new *habit*: to know Jesus →
- A r*eward* → Changed mind (the mind of Christ) →
- Life change

(You may want to go back and re-read the section on page 30: *The Power of Habit*.) *Cues* and *rewards* drive and influence our everyday behaviors. For example, if you highly desire to get fit you start by choosing a simple *cue* such as leaving your workout clothes in the bathroom (or putting a photo of Antonio on the bathroom mirror ☺). Your *reward* is losing a few pounds and a toner physique. When your brain starts expecting *the reward* from the action—working out—it will *trigger a craving*. The brain releases endorphins and then you feel a sense of accomplishment. Only then will it become an automatic *habit* to go to the gym each morning. Cravings power the habit loop.

A new habit requires:

- *Cue* (anything that incites you to act) →
- *Routine* (a repetitive action) →
- *Triggers a craving* in the brain for →
- *Reward* (a perceived value)

Cravings are what drive habits. Therefore, figuring out how to spark a healthy craving makes creating a new habit easier. It makes sense to me that to turn on the mind of Christ we need to crave the *ability to think more like Jesus* (the reward), thereby creating a new habit (routine) by *studying how Jesus thinks*. This is the foundation of mind renewal. This is how it's worked for me:

- *Cue:* My Bible and reading materials are set beside my place mat at the dining room table. (I took a look at my lifestyle and determined that the best time for me to pray and read regularly was early in the morning.) →

- *Routine:* After preparing my breakfast, I sit down at the table and adhere to daily quiet time for Bible reading, prayer and reflection. →

- *Triggers a craving:* I want more of Jesus and the living God; to get closer to God. (As Christians, the Holy Spirit living in us triggers our craving.) →

- *Reward:* Know Him; learn to recognize His voice; and imitate Him. When I pray I speak to God; when I study the Scriptures, He speaks to me. →

- *Daily routine renews my mind (releases endorphins and gives us a sense of accomplishment)* → Transformation.

This routine is what we call "worship." Worship is a spiritual experience that connects our hearts and minds to God. Jesus said, *"But the time is coming—indeed it's here now—when true worshipers will worship the Father in spirit and in truth. The Father is looking for those who will worship him that way" (John 4:23).*

For decades my routine was to make breakfast and either turn on the news or read the newspaper. It was a hard habit to break. So, I weaned myself into it. I started with a 5 to 10-minute commitment to read the Bible and/or a devotional. Then my craving for God grew and the time I spent with Him increased. As the time I spend with God increased, my mind began transforming progressively more.

Keep in mind a healthy reward doesn't always motivate us—*excite us*—to action, like working out. The repetitive action at first doesn't necessarily create a *woo-hoo* moment. Our reward is to be filled with the love and goodness of Jesus which feels different to each person. There are *woo-hoo* moments; there aren't *woo-hoo* moments.

THE 12-MINUTE PHENONIUM

When I created my new habit of worship, this incredible research hadn't been conducted. Scientists have found that *the greatest brain and lifestyle improvements occurred when participants meditated specifically on a loving God for at least 12 minutes per day for 66 days.*[24] This is because our brains have been designed to meditate on truth which enables detachment from emotions like fear and shame and anger. No fitness, self-help, or medical program can do this!

Worshipping God is making a commitment to pray and meditate on Bible verses and testimonies that focus on His love and goodness. This is the prescription for change. Worship can lower overall levels of stress while increasing cognitive alertness and empathy. Steve Arterburn, founder and chairman of *New Life Ministries*, stated that research supports that people who spend at least 4 out of 7 days of the week in God's Word experience *significant transformational change.*

Creating a new healthy habit takes self-discipline. I challenge you for the next month to meditate and hold your thoughts for at least 12 minutes on one or two Scriptures each day. *When God speaks, He packs a lot into His words.* Look up the cross-references in your Bible for context. Ponder what each word means and what God is saying to you. If you don't understand a word, look it up. In a matter of weeks, you'll begin to build and strengthen your relationship with God—and new neural circuits in your brain of compassion and empathy!

HOW LONG? 66/60

We all want to know, "How long will it take to create a new habit?"

It will take, on the average, 63 to 66 days to redesign our brains and form a new habitual thought pattern; and 60 days to break the old pattern.[25] Remember that thoughts are automatized into a habit through deliberate, repeated and conscious thinking. When you repeat a pattern of behavior often enough, eventually you don't have to focus your attention on it anymore (the neural circuits underlying that behavior have stabilized in your brain, enabling you to respond to a similar situation automatically).[26]

Think back to when you learned to drive. At first every move you made was intentional—steering, braking, using the lights and wipers. Before you knew it, you drove automatically. Your ability to drive in America is stored in the *basal ganglia* of your brain, which is why you do it automatically each time you get behind the wheel.

THE TAKE-AWAY

God doesn't seek pious ("holier than thou") prayers or ritualistic practices. He wants nothing but to enjoy time with you, His beloved. When we make it a daily habit to spend time with Jesus, the more like Him we become; the more like Him we think; the more we will experience joy and live the abundant life He spoke of giving us.

Hebrews 12:28 says, *"Therefore, since we are receiving a kingdom that cannot be shaken, let us be thankful, and so worship God acceptably with reverence and awe."*

† *I challenge you to find time each day to turn the world off and seek God. You will find everything you need in Him. Look at your daily habits and pray about what in your day to day schedule needs to be adjusted or changed.*

EAT YOUR FRUIT EVERYDAY

Humanity isn't some random accident. God purposely made us in His image so we might communicate with Him, love Him and be loved by Him (see Genesis 1 & 2). Saint Augustine wrote, "You have made us for yourself, O Lord, and our heart is restless until it finds rest in you."

The good news is God gives us a set of good gifts called "the fruit of the Spirit." Galatians 5:22-23 lists them for us: *love, joy, peace, patience, kindness, goodness, faithfulness, gentleness and self-control.*

God will provide the power to create new healthy habits, and this is what He'll deliver on. Imagine Him pouring each characteristic—each fruit—into your spirit. We particularly need to use *self-control* to make new habitual lifestyle changes. Let's also not forget to be *patient, kind* and *gentle* with ourselves through this process.

STRESSES OF LIFE

Not surprising, researchers have found that creating a new habit works pretty good for most people *until* the stresses of life got too high—such as finding out your mom has cancer, or your marriage is coming apart. It's easy to fall back into old habits. The solution to keeping healthy habits intact is to receive support from others.

Jesus affirmed His followers' need for community (Matthew 18:20). Our culture tends to believe the only way to deeply encounter God is through solitary prayer and study. Jesus implied that His presence will be greatly felt in the presence of a small group. This is why I encourage people to get into the habit of doing Bible studies in a group setting. Doing any life change in a group setting, like Celebrate Recovery or a women's Bible study group, becomes far easier because it occurs in community. Hold each other accountable to keep your new habit going!

7 — STEP TWO: TAKE BIBLICAL ACTION

In Argentina a man decided to transform himself into an elf through plastic surgery. His jaw was broken and reassembled; his chin reshaped; his ears cut open and stretched out; his eyes were made cat-like; and he had four ribs removed to be thinner at the waist. "I have my own beauty ideal and want to achieve that *no matter what*," he said.

This made me think of Justin Jedica who they call "The Human Ken Doll," the guy who's had over 300 plastic surgeries and cosmetic procedures. And let's not forget the women who had near as many procedures to look like a Barbie doll!

God has a better approach to total transformation—not via plastic surgery but by supernatural spiritual renewal. His way doesn't require scalpels or pain or a lot of money. It's free! True transformation isn't from the outside in, but from the inside out.

Once we've made the commitment to develop a new healthy habit of getting closer to God, the next question is: *How does God use the time we give Him to transform our minds?* He tells us through the Bible. Don't believe the devil's lie that you won't be able to understand His Word. The psalmist assures us in Psalm 119:30, *"The teaching of your word gives light, so even the simple can understand."*

1—Romans 12:2: *Don't copy the behavior and customs of this world, but let God transform you into a new person by changing the way you think* [by renewing your mind].

The *world* wants to *control* our minds, but *God* wants to *transform* our minds (see Ephesians 4:17-24; Colossians 3:1-11). He's saying if we allow Him to change the way we think, then we change into a "new person." That's exciting … and a little scary if we're honest.

The only way to be transformed is by the constant renewing of our minds. To "renew" means to "transform to new life." "Transformation" means a change in character. It's an exchange in life—the old mind and old self for the new mind and new self. The word "transform" is the same as "transfigure" in Matthew 17:2. It's come into our English language "metamorphosis" which describes a change from within. The Holy Spirit changes our minds by releasing His power from within.

The math is pretty simple: *Renewed mind = New life.* But we can't overlook our part in this: *Don't copy the behavior and customs of this world.* As we spend more time with God, we will not desire to follow and mimic the ways of the culture.

2—*We demolish arguments and every pretension that sets itself up against the knowledge of God, and we take captive every thought to make it obedient to Christ"* (*2 Corinthians 10:5*).

The Message version: *We use our powerful God-tools for smashing warped philosophies, tearing down barriers erected against the truth of God, fitting every loose thought and emotion and impulse into the structure of life shaped by Christ.*

It can be very difficult to capture and renew something that's already captured us, especially when we're not even aware of it. It may sound daunting, yet when we begin to understand how we can do this, you'll feel confident about change. It begins with asking God to shed light on what's going on in us.

One example: If we're in the middle of an argument with our husband and find ourselves getting emotional and over-reacting, we can stop the conversation before it gets ugly and simply tell him, "I need a time-out to go talk to Jesus." He may be offended, but when he sees Jesus has helped you, he will (he should) freely let you take a time-out in the future.

To "take captive every thought" means we take responsibility for the thought and evaluate against God's Word. It is our spiritual union with Jesus where our power—to demolish—to take captive—to submit and obey—comes from. But it requires creating some new habits. The word "captive" has the meaning of confining or caging up. What thoughts do we have to capture and cage up? *Anything* that goes against God's truth. Simply put: *false beliefs and lies.*

"Quarantine" is a function of antivirus software that isolates infected files on a computer's hard drive. Take a moment and visualize taking an infected deceptive thought out of your mind, then quarantining it (giving it to Jesus). Once quarantined, we replace it with something good, like a thought of gratitude.

If God tells us to do something, He'll give us His power to do it.

3—Ephesians 4:22-24: *You were taught, with regard to your former way of life, to put off your old self, which is being corrupted by its deceitful desires; to be made new in the attitude of your minds; and to put on the new self, created to be like God in true righteousness and holiness.*

1 Corinthians 2:16: *We have the mind of Christ.*

It's been said that there's no such thing as a gray sky. The sky is always blue. However, sometimes gray clouds come out and cover up the blue sky. It's like that with our minds. We have the perfect mind of Christ—a powerful sound mind—yet it gets clouded with fearful patterns and distorted beliefs.

When we are born into the kingdom of God, called "born-again," everything is different—our position has changed. *You are a new creation (2 Corinthians 5:17)* living in union with Jesus Christ (Col. 2:6-7; John 14:20). We have to learn a new way to think, act and feel. The Bible calls this our "new self." All the while we're fighting the inner tendencies and beliefs (which have been *corrupted by its deceitful desires*) that we've clung to for decades.

God invites us to take our messy baggage to Him and leave it at the foot of the cross. He doesn't hold the past against us. What does this tell you about God?

Note all the verbs in these three Scriptures; words that are intended to illicit a response and some kind of action from us:

- Don't copy
- Let God transform
- Demolish
- Make it obedient
- Put off | Put on
- Be made new

Sometimes we're either puzzled by a command or wonder how we can possibly do it. Then we're tempted to ignore it. Even when we don't understand completely, we can trust God to know His instructions are for our own good. He has our best interests at heart and knows the consequences of not doing what He asks.

Only by learning to "put off" the garbage—the *arguments and every pretension that sets itself up against the knowledge of God; the corrupted deceitful desires,* and "put on" the *mind of Christ*—can we truly experience the freedom to break our false masks and reprogram the routines in our lives. We live *created to be like God in true righteousness and holiness.* God's will for us is to be transformed into Christ's image. It is the goal and purpose of our lives as Christians.

Considering our minds are filled with beliefs and memories going back to infancy, this seems near impossible. Paul explains how the impossible is turned into the possible:

4—Ephesians 1:17-20; 3:20: *I keep asking that the God of our Lord Jesus Christ, the glorious Father, may* **give you the Spirit of wisdom** *and revelation, so that* **you may know him better.** *I pray also that the eyes of your heart may be enlightened in order that you may know the hope to which he has called you, the riches of his glorious inheritance in the saints, and* **his incomparably great power for us who believe.** *That power is like the working of his mighty strength,* *which he exerted in Christ when he raised him from the dead and seated him at his right hand in the heavenly realms. ... He is able to do immeasurably more than all we ask or imagine,* **according to his power that is at work within us**" *(Ephesians 3:20).*

2 Timothy 1:7: *For God hath not given us the spirit of fear; but of* **power,** *and of love, and of a* **sound mind** *(KJV).*

The Greek word for "power" is *dunamis* as in "dynamo" and "dynamite." Paul is telling us that God's divine, dynamic and eternal energy is available to us. God shares with His creation a portion of His own power. This is the power which transforms our minds into the mind of Christ. Then something miraculous happens as His power begins to transform our minds—*"you will know the truth, and the truth will set you free" (John 8:32).*

God knows how desperately we need to be set free from the lies we believe about ourselves, others and Him. With Jesus's mind operating in us as our mind's hard drive, He can penetrate deep and expose, cleanse and heal toxic areas, while rooting out the strongholds of the enemy; exposing the darkness and bringing truth and light into our life when we *put Jesus in the center* of our lives.

It was only by sitting at the feet of Jesus and getting to know Him intimately, did His disciple's minds change profoundly. We can't physically sit with Him today, but we can learn from Him through the Gospels and by creating a spiritually intimate relationship.

I challenge you for the next month to meditate and hold your thoughts for at least 12 minutes each day on one of these Scriptures. (Recall: 12 minutes of daily focused prayer over an 8-week period can change the brain to such an extent that it can be measured on a brain scan.[27]) If you are seriously meditating and pondering on what God is trying to tell you, you may find you spend several days on just one Scripture. He's given us a lot to chew on.

Gray clouds don't last; blue sky does. As Jesus begins to teach us how to take every thought captive, we can get free of, not only our conscious negative thoughts and emotions, but also all the unconscious *hidden secret* doubts, fears, bitterness, shame, anxieties, unforgiveness, unbelief and insecurities that we've buried deep within our souls—those things which have driven us for most of our lives. Then His life and Love flows through us in a new and powerful way.

† *Ask yourself: What is God telling me in this material? What am going to do about it?*

8 — STEP THREE: BELIEVE

Say this out loud: "I have the mind of Christ!" Do you feel like you have His mind? Would those closest to you testify that based on how you act that you have put on the mind of Christ?

It's time to really believe it. First Corinthians 2 affirms that if we are a Christian (which means we have saving faith in Jesus Christ and the Holy Spirit indwells and enlightens us) then we possess the mind of Christ. *"The LORD declared, "I will put my law in their minds …* "Law" in Hebrew (*torah*) primarily means "teaching" or "instruction." Jeremiah 31:33 is saying that God puts His instructions on how to live a godly life in our minds. Most of us have been ignorant not just to what the mind of Christ is, but also what it does and how it works. Therefore, we haven't been able to use this incredible powerful gift God has given us. As a result, we continue to depend on old faulty thoughts, beliefs and emotions—playing right into the enemy's hand.

This is exactly what happened to me for the first 14-years I lived as a Christian. I believed all I had to do was go to church once a week. I was ignorant to what God's Word said because I chose not to study it; I felt it was irrelevant. Since my thinking patterns and belief system didn't change; I didn't change. I continued to live as a worldly Christian.

You may be thinking, *What's wrong with my thinking? It's served me pretty well so far.* Isaiah 55:8 states, *""For my thoughts are not your thoughts, neither are your ways my ways," declares the LORD."* Isaiah tells us that our own natural thinking is not only different from God's, but usually the total opposite. We're not even aware that our own thinking is different and counter-cultural to His. Haven't you found this to be true as you have started studying Gods Word?

Just because we are Christians doesn't mean we *automatically* think God's thoughts with the mind of Christ. It is when we come before Him and ask as David did, *"Clean the slate, God, so we can start the day fresh! Keep me from stupid sins, from thinking I can take over your work" (Psalm 19:12; MSG).*

QUEEN RAVENNA KIND OF THOUGHTS

Ever see the movie *Snow White and the Huntsman* based on the fairy tale *Snow White and the Seven Dwarfs?* The evil witch, Queen Ravenna, periodically drains the youth from the kingdom's young women in order to maintain her power, which allows her to keep her youthful beauty. Honestly, I relate to her desire to want to remain youthful. I fight the fact that my mature aging body makes me feel invisible to the rest of the outside world. Might I be feeling as if my security blanket has been taken away from me? I admit I liked being given a second look. I'm not alone. It's a cultural issue for any woman over 40 living in America. Ladies, can't we say that we've ended up living a gigantic lie?

When God says to take every thought captive, He doesn't mean examine every single thought we have. He means stop and take a good look at the anxious, hurtful, self-centered deceptive and doubtful ones; the anger, pride, jealousy and all the other "emotional baggage" kind of thoughts—the Queen Ravenna kind of thoughts. This means asking the Holy Spirit to clarify whether that thought will help us or hurt us. Once I started interrogating my thoughts and actions versus blowing them off, God was able to expose and clean out a lot of old junk and hurts.

You ask, "How can I tell if God is speaking to me about my thoughts? Great question! This is the way I see it.

1—God's promptings come in a still, small voice that bears witness with our spirit. We will usually feel immediate confirmation and peace.

2—God's voice will always be in perfect agreement with His Word, the Holy Bible.

3—I ask myself, "If Jesus were physically standing here beside me right now, do I strongly believe this is what He'd be whispering in my ear?

Thoughts that are not from God have two other sources: the flesh and Satan (which we'll be covering shortly). Some of our thoughts that God exposes will disappear immediately, while other He exposes are long-standing "strongholds" which won't let go easily. Don't be dismayed or discouraged if these keep reoccurring. With time and a commitment to follow God's practices, they can disappear.

† *Elaborate on what it means to you to have "the mind of Christ." Share any personal stories where acting on the mind of Christ enhanced your experience with God and/or others.*

9 — STEP FOUR:
TAKE UP YOUR NEW POSITION

When I was in second grade, our family moved from America to England. Nothing was normal any more—new words and accents, a new way of dressing, new sights and sounds, new traditions and values. On the first day of school I had gym class. Unbeknownst to our family, the boys and girls had gym together. Each child was clothed in uniform underwear—dark navy-blue knickers (British for underpants) and a thick, stark white undershirt.

I slithered into the gym wearing a flimsy undershirt with a cute little bow and worn out, flowery panties with a big old hole along the elastic line! The kids snickered and laughed at me. I was devastated. I wanted so badly to go back to America—to the familiar and habitual. Desperate to fit in, eventually I took hold of their customs.

The truth is our new born-again Christian self still lives in our old body (Romans 7:21-25). What many of us fail to realize is that our old nature and old ways of thinking don't instantly disappear when we become a believer. The old way is comfortable and takes less effort because it's ingrained in our flesh and programmed into our minds. We don't automatically think good godly thoughts and express the right attitudes. We don't get a new personality. We are new in Christ but still live in the same world, with the same family, in the same body, with all those old memories, desires, habits and consequences called the "old self."

Becoming a Christian doesn't remove the internal impulse to sin nor does it deter the devil from trying to exploit it. What we can do is draw on the power that God so generously gives us so we can resist these influences and begin changing our thinking patterns. Every Christian has the mind of Christ, but not every Christian will be able to use it *unless* they recognize that their own way of thinking and feeling is opposite from God's, and they recognize the importance of taking each questionable and worldly thought captive.

If we can discern things from God's vantage point, then we'll be able to rise above our circumstances instead of continually getting buried under them. When our lives change, then we are in the position to bless God. *"Bless the LORD, O my soul …"* (Psalm 103:1). Isn't that what we all really want—to bless God?

The Message paraphrase of Romans 12:2 reminds us to put into practice, through the empowerment of the Holy Spirit, several things:

> *Don't become so well-adjusted to your culture that you fit into it without even thinking. Instead,* **fix your attention on God.** *You'll be changed from the inside out.* **Readily recognize what he wants from you,** *and* **quickly respond to it.** *Unlike the culture around you, always dragging you down to its level of immaturity, God brings the best out of you, develops well-formed maturity in you.*

MIND CHANGE = BRAIN CHANGE

When our minds change, our habits change, our brains change, and then our lives change. Brain scans show something remarkable happens: There is new activity in the region of the brain where they believe behavioral inhibition and self-discipline starts. Neurological patterns—old worthless habits, for example—are overridden by new worthwhile patterns. Scientists can still see neural activity of old behaviors but those impulses were crowded out by new urges and new patterns. And this change gets more pronounced as transformation occurs.[28]

If you decide to move forward let me warn you: You are entering a battlefield for your mind. This process takes *desire, discipline* and making some *sacrifices.* Sometimes it will seem easier to give up and let the wild emotions continue to rule. I encourage you to think of several instances where you've successfully used discipline and/or sacrificed to accomplish something important to you. You can do this! *You have the power to take your mind back because you have the mind of Christ!*

I could close this study right here and say, "You've now got the four steps to mind transformation. Go and put them into practice." If I do that then I haven't given you enough tools to fill your toolbox. I've given you the essentials like the hammer, screwdriver, tape measure and wrench, but as every handyman will tell you, to do the job right you need several kinds of screwdrivers and wrenches, some pliers and a drill. This is what I'm going to do—give you some more tools to ensure you are successful, or as the Bible would say, "fruitful." But I also need to be clear—God and His Word defines our mind renewal plan—not me nor you.

The Believer's Conflict Zones

The temptations in your life are no different from what others experience. And God is faithful. He will not allow the temptation to be more than you can stand. When you are tempted, he will show you a way out so that you can endure.

—1 Corinthians 10:13

10 — LIFE'S NEGATIVE INFLUENCES

There's a bumper sticker that says, "Life never seems to turn out the way you think it will 90 % of the time." As Christians we hear talk of joy and freedom, but often wonder "where is it?" We've got impressive, timesaving computers and gadgets, yet we're over-scheduled and over-stressed because there aren't enough hours in the day to do everything we want. Add to that whiney teenagers, insensitive spouses, harried commutes and financial challenges—life gets increasingly fractured and broken. It's a picture of people in bondage.

"Bondage" is the opposite of freedom. Freedom, according to Americans, means I do what it takes to make me happy. I'm independent, self-reliant and self-indulgent. Take this married woman for example. She won two tickets to Hawaii for a couple. She ecstatically exclaimed, "Yay! I get to go to Hawaii twice!" (With an attitude like this perhaps her husband would have been pleased for her to go alone.)

We cannot spend day after day in this world without it affecting our minds, our hearts and our souls. They become unguarded. Our hearts shift away from God. We aren't even aware this is happening. We go about our business believing all is well, but deep down inside something feels wrong. David cried to God, *"How long must I wrestle with my thoughts and every day have sorrow in my heart? How long will my enemy triumph over me?" (Psalm 13:2)*. His soul is conflicted.

Most people are totally unaware there are 3 areas in our lives where conflict consistently arises:

- Through the *world*—a system of different and/or unhealthy values and morals.
- Directly through *Satan* and his demons.
- Through our own *flesh*—within *ourselves;* our *ego*.

These negative influences commonly work together to lead people away from God, while negatively affecting their beliefs, thinking and behavior. It can be hard to discern when our struggles are a result of the devil's intervention, us acting in our flesh, environmental stress, or even abnormal brain physiology. To grow, we must acknowledge them and learn how to resist them.

CONFLICT WITH THE WORLD

In 1978, some 900 members of the People's Temple cult committed mass suicide by drinking a mixture of grape Kool-Aid laced with Valium and Cyanide. These poor souls never imagined that joining this group for spiritual growth and social justice would end in suicide. A University of Oregon commentator responded,

> The sad truth is that they had already drunk the Kool-Aid long before they took their own lives, by killing off their ability to think critically and independently. Humans are endowed with extraordinary powers of observation and analysis, and yet we are also susceptible to deep-seeded desires for acceptance and conformity.[29]

"Deep-seeded desires for acceptance and conformity" touch everyone in many different ways. And "the world" thinks it has the answers. The world places people, self (and self-beliefs) and things at the center of one's ambitions and activities.

"Secular" usually means "belonging to this age or this world." Worldliness, or secularism, is the ungodly aspects of our culture, like what is in, what is uncool, customs, philosophies and attitudes. Our disposition, temperament and habits are manipulated through the world—the workplace, social media and entertainment, advertising, the education system, peer groups, and world views. Today smartphones, social media and gaming devours people's time, and like stimulants, numbs the brain's pleasure center.[30] No doubt our minds are more at risk now than ever before.

Lois Tverberg, author of *Sitting at the Feet of Jesus*, wrote,

I find that my own mind seems remarkably malleable, impressed by whatever I read or see modeled around me. A steady diet of cynical political commentary always makes me more negative. Being with friends who gossip can make me more careless about how I speak. None of us is so mature that we cannot be influenced. The question is: Who or what do we want to shape our lives? Even the culture around us will try to 'disciple' us if we have not placed ourselves under the transforming influence of Jesus Christ.

When we worship and let ourselves be influenced by worldly things over God it becomes "idolatry" which God considers a sin (Deut. 4:15-19). Our culture promotes "me first" and then others *if* anything is left over. That's *I-dolatry*—a world enchanted with ourselves and disenchanted with God (a big reason relationships break down). Secularism has *"exchanged the truth of God for a lie and worshiped and served the creature rather than the Creator" (Romans 1:25)*.

The world, as presented in John 1:1-18, is all that is opposed to Jesus Christ. These influences contribute to the breakdown of the family, addictions, adultery, pornography and abuse. Sadly, many Christians are not all that different from the world. It's been said that many people are willing to be God-centered as long as God is man-centered. We say we want Jesus—but we don't want His kind of transformation. Solomon, the wisest man in the world, wrote,

So, after a lot of thinking, I decided to try the road of drink, while still holding steadily to my course of seeking wisdom. Next I changed my course again and followed the path of folly, so that I could experience the only happiness most men have throughout their lives. Then I tried to find fulfillment by inaugurating a great public works program: homes, vineyards, gardens, parks, and orchards for myself, and reservoirs to hold the water to irrigate my plantations. Next I bought slaves, both men and women, and others were born within my household. I also bred great herds and flocks, more than any of the kings before me. I collected silver and gold as taxes from many kings and provinces. In the cultural arts, I organized men's and women's choirs and orchestras. And then there were my many beautiful concubines. So I became greater than any of the kings in Jerusalem before me, and with it all I remained clear-eyed, so that I could evaluate all these things. Anything I wanted I took and did not restrain myself from any joy. I even found great pleasure in hard work. This pleasure was, indeed, my only reward for all my labors. But as I looked at everything I had tried, it was all so useless, a chasing of the wind, and there was nothing really worthwhile anywhere (Ecclesiastes 2:3-11).

What stands out to you in this passage?

Did you notice he used the word "I" eight times, and in the end, he inferred it wasn't worth it—"was all so useless." If we follow the world's ways, we miss God's blessings. This is why the Bible tells us:

- *Don't love the world's ways. Don't love the world's goods. Love of the world squeezes out love for the Father (1 John 2:15, MSG).*
- *To be a friend of the world is to become an enemy of God (James 4:4).*
- *You cannot serve two masters: God and money. For you will hate one and love the other, or else the other way around (Matthew 6:24).*

I challenge you to carefully assess where the world may be influencing your values and behavior in a less than Christian way. Ask yourself:

- Am I being shaped more by the secular spirit of the world or by the Spirit of God?

- Do people's opinions determine my choices?
- How do I invest my financial resources (telling about what we consider important)?
- Do I feel it's important to cultivate genuine care and concern for others (telling about how selfish we are)?

Dallas Willard wrote, "Few people arise in the morning as hungry for God as they are for cornflakes or toast and eggs." We'll give quality time to a friend, a therapist, a class, a pastor or a doctor. We'll find time to eat, but we're not very good at giving quality time to God, the one who really nourishes us.

† *Someone said, "If the world controls your thinking—you are a conformer. If God controls it, you are transformer." How committed are you to be a transformer?*

1	2	3	4	5	6	7	8	9	10
Not committed									Extremely committed

11 — MEET THE ACCUSER

Perhaps you've caught reruns of the popular Sci-Fi series *The Twilight Zone.* "You are about to enter another dimension, a dimension not only of sight and sound but of mind. A journey into a wondrous land of imagination. Next stop, the Twilight Zone!"

When we speak of the supernatural and the invisible, it feels like the twilight zone. However, the Bible is clear this dimension is not of our imagination. It is real. And there exists a real evil being the Bible calls Satan.

There are many popular ideas about Satan. Some think Satan is not real but rather a personification of the wickedness that abides in the world, or just plain baloney. Many Christians who believe in Satan do not identify him as being the enemy of their personal lives. Or, they believe because they are Christian, they cannot be affected. This is a lie. If Satan doesn't attack Christians, why are we instructed in Ephesians 6:1 to put on the full armor of God so that we will be able to stand safe against all strategies and tricks of Satan?

YOUR ENEMY

Pleased to meet you
Hope you guessed my name, oh yeah
But what's confusing you
Is just the nature of my game, mm yeah
—Sympathy for the Devil by the Rolling Stones

The Bible records that long ago, God's kingdom was challenged by an angel named Satan. In Hebrew it is pronounced *Sah-tahn* and translates as "accuser" or "adversary." He is the most powerful of fallen angels, also referred to as *the devil, Lucifer, the great deceiver, the tempter, the destroyer, accuser of the brethren, a monstrous dragon* and *evil one.* Scripture is clear "the enemy" isn't one demon but an entire legion of evil spirits following Satan's commands (Mark 5:1-20).

The Bible reveals little about his sinful fall from heaven. At his fall, Satan established a counterfeit kingdom. Ephesians 2:21 calls him the *"prince of the power of the air."* He has power over the earth where he and his demons move and exist. Satan's motive was, and still is, to claim authority over this earth. One minister I know takes this verse literally to mean he has power over the communication airways, which explains why conservatives contend the media is "fake" and biased.

What most people don't realize is our world is under Satan's control. He is referred to as the *god of this age* (2 Corinthians 4:4) and *the ruler of this world* (John 12:31; 1 John 5:19). Consider this illustration.

There is a large group of people and a fence. On one side of the fence stood Jesus; on the other side Satan. Each person had to choose to go with either Jesus or Satan. Jesus gathered His group and so did Satan. But one man joined neither group. He climbed the fence and sat on it.

Jesus and His people left and so did Satan and his people. The man just sat alone on the fence. Then Satan came back. (Have you noticed he always comes back?)

The man said, "Have you lost something?"

Satan replied, "No, there you are. Come with me."

The man said, "I sat on the fence. I chose neither you nor Him."

To which Satan replied, "Come with me. I own the fence."

When we believe Satan controls the entire world—and God is not the author of evil—then we look at the question: "Why do bad things happen to good people?" in an entirely new light. We're kind of amazed there's any goodness left at all in the world.

The Bible tells us,

For we are not fighting against flesh-and-blood enemies, but against evil rulers and authorities of the unseen world, against mighty powers in this dark world, and against evil spirits in the heavenly places (Ephesians 6:12).

The Message reads: *This is no afternoon athletic contest that we'll walk away from and forget about in a couple of hours. This is for keeps, a life-or-death fight to the finish against the Devil and all his angels.*

Satan is like a terrorist out to demolish, corrupt the human mind, even kill, believers (John 10:10; 1 Peter 5:7). He hates all that God loves, which is us. His objective is to influence individuals to disobey God and sin; to tarnish God's holy name. He does this by somehow perverting all God has created as good, beautiful and moral.

Sadly, few Christians in America take teachings about Satan seriously. This is like saying you believe some of the Bible is truth and the rest is made up.

† *What have you been taught about Satan and do you believe it?*

SATAN'S FAVORITE TARGET

In the 1950s and 1960s, missionary (Saint) Mother Teresa wrote several letters, which were revealed after her death to her church spiritual guides. The letters disclosed troubling and painful conflicts she sometimes had with her faith.

"I am told God lives in me—and yet the reality of darkness and coldness and emptiness is so great that nothing touches my soul," she wrote in one of the letters. Some of the letters depict a spiritually bereaved Mother Teresa, struggling to maintain her belief.

"Where I try to raise my thoughts to heaven, there is such convicting emptiness that those very thoughts return like sharp knives and hurt my very soul. Love—the word—it brings nothing," wrote the woman known as the "Messiah of Love." In another letter, Mother Teresa wrote, "In my soul, I can't tell you how dark it is, how painful, how terrible—I feel like refusing God."[31]

Because of Mother Teresa's powerful and life-changing ministry and world-wide recognition, we can be certain Satan was firing toxic missiles at her mind to discourage and disarm her.

Satan is dedicated to preventing our transformation into Christlikeness (*Christlike* means God manifested in and through us; our flesh). He knows if he can keep us ignorant as to how to transform our minds God's way, then we'll go on depending on our own self-centered thoughts, remaining conformed to the world's image and not Jesus's. He does this by keeping us in bondage to our old ways of thinking. This is why our mind is Satan's most frequent target of attacks (1 Chronicles 21:1; John 13.2). The second reason he attacks our minds is because our minds are the part of the image of God where God communicates with us and reveals His will to us (Luke 11:17; Romans 12:2; Eph. 4:23-24).

Unknowingly, we Christians embrace the devil's mind games and accept them as truth. Jesus said, *"The devil was a murderer from the beginning, not holding to the truth, for there is no truth in him for he is a liar and the father of all lies" (John 8:44).* Lies are very powerful. If Satan can get you to believe a lie, then he can begin to work in your life to lead you away from God and into sin. When we believe the devil's lie instead of God's words of truth, we are powerless to do what is right.

CHERIE'S MISINTERPRETATION

Cherie was told all of her life that she'd never amount to anything. She claimed everything she touched fell apart. One day she was reading in Romans, *"Does not the potter have the right to make out of the same lump of clay some pottery for noble purposes and some for common use?" (Romans 9:21)*

Cherie interpreted the verse to mean that God intentionally creates some people to be blessed and successful and others to be cursed and failures. She believed she was the latter. Scripture confirmed what her family had told her all her life. She believed a lie that came right out of the Bible.

Cherie knew the potter was God, but what she didn't know was that Paul was addressing a group of Christians who mixed pride, bigotry and fleshly works with Christ's Word. Paul's desire was to wean his readers away from self-sufficiency. Paul was telling the Romans that we humans have no basis to question the acts of God. We lack the capacity to grasp God's infinite mind or the way He intervenes in our lives. He is not accountable to us.

This interpretation is 180 degrees apart from Cherie's understanding. Satan always masquerades his lies as God's truth. Second Corinthians 11:14 states, *"Satan himself masquerades as an angel of light."* He enjoys taking verses out of context to create false beliefs. This is why it is so important to have a proper grasp of Scripture. It is important that when we start our study of the Scriptures, in addition to our own individual study time, we are learning from reputable pastors and teachers. Solomon wisely advised: *"For lack of guidance a nation falls, but many advisers make victory sure" (Proverbs 11:14)*.

The Sting of a Thought Dart

Katelyn believed she put her past behind her. Then something would trigger an old memory and the toxic thoughts, the guilt and self-condemnation, would come spilling out like an oil gusher.

When was the last time you felt the sting of a "thought dart" that suddenly attacked your mind out of nowhere? *Huh?*

Paul told the Ephesians to take up the "shield of faith" in order to extinguish all the "flaming arrows" of the evil one (Ephesians 6:16). The flaming arrows he is speaking of are aimed right at our mind. Another biblical term is "fiery darts" symbolic of fiery trials or temptations; of distractions or storms; or toxic, evil thoughts. I call them *thought darts*.

Satan's intent is to plant a suggestion snowball, which grows in size. Negative thoughts have a snowball effect which can immobilize us. Just one can lead into a mild case of the blues, which can turn into a general fog, then depression. He somehow plants a suggestion in the form of a temptation, an accusation, deception and the urge to sin. *You'll never be able to do that. You've failed miserably in the past. They'll just laugh at you. A couple glasses of wine will decrease your anxiety.*

Let me also say: As you go through this study, if you start feeling defeated, as in "This isn't working for me," that's exactly what Satan desires. Satan's voice is different from God's. It's more a demanding voice, planting an urgent "Do it now" kind of thought, often prompting strife, doubt and confusion.

Elsie said, "When I have PMS, that's when I hear Satan's voice the loudest." Maybe you can relate. Recognize you're in a battle with him. *You will win* if you persevere. Recall James 4:7, *"Submit yourselves, then, to God. Resist the devil, and he will flee from you."*

Get Off the Fence

Many ask how Satan does this. Can he read our minds? We know God knows our thoughts (Luke 11:17), but there is nothing in the Bible to indicate that Satan can read our thoughts. The Bible never says demons or angels are all-knowing (omniscient). They are created beings. Satan is adept at predicting human behavior because of his immense knowledge of mankind. Somehow, he can predict what you and I may do in a given situation without knowing our thoughts.

Today, many of us feel the battle wounds from those thought darts—the discouragement, depression, anxiety, fear, shame, anger and guilt. After a dart hits, our body reacts. As we have learned, the human body is loaded with many different kinds of chemicals and hormones released by our brain in response to our thoughts. Whenever you think awful, miserable, negative thoughts, your brain works less efficiently and is likely to put you into an emotional and physical slump.[32]

All behavior starts with that one thought. One negative or toxic thoughts → toxic feeling → toxic attitude → toxic behavior. Every addiction, every felony and every adulterous affair started with one deceptive lie. Satan whispers, *No big deal! You can get away with this. You're not really sinning!* After we sin, he laughs. *Idiot! You'll never get away with this. You better go self-medicate and isolate.*

This is a further reason mind renewal is so critical—because whoever directs and controls our thinking is ultimately the one who will direct and control our lives. We can't just sit on the fence. By agreeing with his lies, we enable the devil to *"kill, steal, and destroy" (John 10:10)*. No wonder 1 Peter 5:8 warns us: *"Stay alert! Watch out for your great enemy, the devil. He prowls around like a roaring lion, looking for someone to devour."*

I don't know about you, but I want to learn all I can from God and godly people so I'm not his lunch!

✝ *Describe a time when you have been immobilized or acted ungodly due to a toxic thought dart penetrating your mind.*

†††

True story: Preacher Rowland Hill was preaching to a crowd of people when the wealthy aristocrat, Lady Ann Erskine, drove up in her coach. Seeing her, the reverend changed his sermon.

He declared, "I have something for sale. It is the soul of Lady Erskine. Do I hear a bid? Who bids? Satan bids. Satan, what will you give for her soul? 'I will give riches, honor and pleasure.' ... But stop, do I hear another bid? Yes, it's Jesus Christ. Jesus, what will You give for her soul? 'I give her eternal life.' Lady Erskine, you've heard the two bids, which will you take?"

Lady Erskine, realizing Jesus purchased her soul with His blood, chose Jesus.[33]

12 –THE LYING SERPENT AND THE FALL

A FBI agent specializing in behavioral analysis wrote, "Most people—both laypersons and professionals—are not very good at detecting lies. Identifying deceit is so difficult. ... Truth is essential for all relations."[34]

We learn to lie when we're children. We're taught things like, "Tell them we're not home," or "Put on a happy smile." Even cosmetics and body shaping clothing, like push-up bras and Spanx, are designed to deceive.

Today the deceiver, Satan, successfully trips us all up by getting us to believe lies—twisted truths, half-truths and total lies. (A *lie* is simply the denial, repression, perversion or distortion of the truth.) Through lying, he gets us to question and doubt who God really is and who we are. Those lies are then passed down through the generations.

Satan's objective is to present the bait and hide the hook. By this devise, he took mankind's first parents, Adam and Eve, which is how this mess began (read Genesis 3). For reasons that will never be clear, our fore-parents listened to Satan, disguised as a slithering gnarly serpent. He lied declaring that their Creator wasn't essentially good, but instead an exploiter.

By choosing to ignore God's command and listen to the lying serpent, the couple willfully disobeyed God. When they believed his lie, they naively joined his rebellion and turned from God. Before, they were called to co-reign with God. But when they "ate" they placed themselves under the serpent's lie, severing the world from God and unleashing the deceiver's destructive power into God's good world. And once this mistrust possessed their minds and hearts, fear set in.

The debacle with Adam and Eve is what theologians call "the fall"—the fall of mankind. Consequently, lies, fear, shame and other toxic emotions emerged. And our brains and minds got turned off to the Creator's plan. Today Satan doesn't present himself as a snake. But he slithers into our lives through other avenues like addictions, advertising, games, social media, movies (like *Fifty Shades of Grey*), psychics and influential people.

By giving His created a free will, God allows us to choose, and therefore, to reap the dire penalties of our own rebellious choices. Scripture says God's children exchanged the truth of God for a lie, and therefore, God gave them over to a "depraved mind" and the sinful desires of their hearts (Romans 1:25, 28). Basically, God said, "I told you blessings come with obedience, but if you don't want that, go ahead and do your own thing. Let's see what happens!"

"Depraved" means that everyone, even a child, is affected by sin, in everything they do. A foolish and evil mind is described frequently in Scripture. The Bible states that the sinful tendencies of the fathers are passed from generation to generation (Exodus 20:5).

Pastor and author Louie Giglio, speaking of generational sin, said,

Our parents are the product of Adam. And the product of Adam's sin is a fallen race and your parents are dominoes in that chain of events. And so, when you came into the world, you came into the world as a product of a fallen mother and a fallen father. Even if they were believers in Christ, even if they've been born again, they still were carrying the DNA of sin in their lives.[35]

Let me say: To those *who do not know* God and His Word, the voices of God and the devil are scarcely distinguishable. This is why God says its critical to take every thought captive—to capture, expose and examine it. We've got to see where our thoughts are coming from and determine if the voice is God's, our ego's or Satan's.

BRAIN DYSFUNCTION

Another calamitous result of the fall, is our brains are out of balance. Today, in most people, the pleasure center in the brain is abused, over-stimulated or taxed beyond its capacities. As I said before, our brains have been turned off from the Creator's plan. The result: We can't find real joy, even the joy that comes from God.

Dr. Archibald Hart states that our pursuit of pleasure has skyrocketed. He wrote,

> Today we are relentlessly pushing the pleasure button in our brains and overloading a system that is not designed to be continuously stimulated. The result is *anhedonia*, a condition in which our brain slowly loses the capacity to give us real pleasure.[36]

There is a "joy center" in our brains. (It is a scientific term.) It is the only area of the brain that grows throughout the life cycle. Every other area of our brain has peak periods and then starts to decline. The joy center is responsible for emotional joy, rest and balance.

When we optimize our joy center, we thrive, our relationships thrive, and we live from the new heart Jesus gave us.[37]

One of the leading (Christian) psychiatrists in this country, Dr. Timothy Jennings, states in his book *The God Shaped Brain,* that when our brains are out of balance, consequently:

- We experience the effects of free-flowing anxiety, out-of-control stress, fear and selfishness. →
- The *amygdala* part of the brain (which processes memory, decision-making and emotional reactions) fires up continuously. →
- Fear circuits are activated and stress circuits are reactive. →
- Produces chronic inflammation and damage to both our brains and bodies. →
- Love, growth, development and healthy thinking decrease.

The other consequence of believing a distorted view of God is our eternal salvation depends on our beliefs. If we believe God is the bad guy, then we'll not likely accept the gospel message and will not be saved eternally. Now can you see why it's critical we know the truth about God?

Dr. Jennings claims that when we consistently believe lies—for example, lies about God, such as, "He is a tyrant and doesn't care about me;" or "He can't wait to send me to hell;" or lies about ourselves, such as, "I'm a loser and no one could ever love me," what happens is:

- Unhealthy neural circuits in the brain get fired up and grow stronger. →
- The *prefrontal cortex* of the brain is damaged (where thoughts and actions are coordinated). →
- Results in a selfish, fear-controlled brain. →
- Stress levels rise because fear is the root of stress. →
- Love is impaired; therefore, relationships are damaged. →
- We are prevented from living the lives God desires.

False beliefs and lies change neural circuits in our brains which damage our minds and characters. Brain science has documented that *what you believe about God changes your brain—either positively or negatively*. Believing lies, especially about God, obstructs the transformation and healing process. This is because the selfish, fear-controlled brain is resistant to God.[38] When we seek to know the truth and the real true God of the Holy Bible—the God who loves us unconditionally and wants to lavish His love, mercy, grace and forgiveness upon us—the God who wants to heal and transform us—then the neural circuitry in our brains is changed positively. This is scientifically proven.

The bottom line is this: *God loves us with an everlasting love. But the rejection of that love separates us from its life-giving power, resulting in disintegration and death.* When love and truth pour into our lives and minds, not only does fear decrease, but growth, development and healthy thinking improves which means our characters and our lives are changed!

† *Describe any similarities or patterns you see in your life.*

GOD'S PLAN

"The fall" means that God's intimacy with man was lost. Imagine it: Before the couple sinned, God made earth His home, walking with Adam and Eve. But after sin entered the picture, God left for heaven, giving the earth to us. Like the prodigal son in Jesus's famous parable, we asked the Father for our inheritance—not to enjoy it together with Him, but to squander it on ourselves. God generously gave mankind his and her wish. He handed us over to what we wanted—a world without Him.

Their decision had cosmic consequences. However, the Creator compassionately loves His creation and provided a way out. *The LORD looked down from his sanctuary on high, from heaven he viewed the earth, to hear the groans of the prisoners and release those condemned to death (Psalm 102:19-20).*

This is why Jesus had to come—to rescue mankind. As theologian Tom Wright puts it, Jesus had to go to the very eye of the storm, to the place where evil was doing its worst and offer Himself, His own life, as the means of defeating evil at last. *"God did this according to his eternal plan. And he was able to do what he had planned because of all Christ Jesus our Lord had done"* (Ephesians 3:11; CEV).

All this was for you and me. On the cross Christ suffered the most excruciating physical, emotional and spiritual torture in order to deliver us from the curse of sin—of abuse, fear, shame and selfishness. It was the only way. It may have looked like God checked out and evil won. But God has been very much at work.

Jesus did the beautiful work of buying back our lost souls in the most amazing act of grace and mercy and love ever seen. He literally undid the sin of Adam. Jesus literally took our sinful rebellious sick condition on Himself in order to restore humanity and immortal life back to God's original design. This act shows how important and valuable we are to God.

Jesus reconnected mankind with the Father and restored the flow of life and love. Satan's only remaining strategy is to continue to spread lies about God—lies that when believed prevent us from trusting God and receiving the gospel message.

Romans 8:29-30 in The Message states,

God knew what he was doing from the very beginning. He decided from the outset to shape the lives of those who love him along the same lines as the life of his Son. The Son stands first in the line of humanity he restored. We see the original and intended shape of our lives there in him. After God made that decision of what his children should be like, he followed it up by calling people by name. After he called them by name, he set them on a solid basis with himself. And then, after getting them established, he stayed with them to the end, gloriously completing what he had begun.

✝ *What is God saying to you in through this beautiful passage? What does it mean to you personally?*

13 – MEET FLESH WOMAN

Have you noticed the American culture socializes girls differently than boys? One defining difference is the greater emphasis on physical attractiveness and appearance for girls. Just go into a baby's clothing store—way more cute girl clothes than boy clothes. It's as if women in our culture grow up to develop—at a very early age—two distinct self-identities: their body and their mind. Society seems to say, "It's better to be pretty than smart." Boys are given Legos and science kits to "build their minds." In other words, a typical female's mind suffers at the expense of her body.

For 20-years I lived that American girl existence, living addicted to body-image, exercise, food, cigarettes, diet pills—things I believed would create a perfect body. I believed these "gods"—beauty and success—had what I was searching for because life was "all about me." It lacked joy and hope; only fear, shame and self-condemnation.

Dr. John Bargh, in his book *Before You Know It*, in speaking of why we are addicted to things like dieting, exercise and tanning, stated these things help us achieve a "mating goal." We do these things to make us feel more attractive to other's.[39] I wouldn't say we only do these things to attract a mate; we desire to look attractive to get people's attentions, to get a good job, etc. He made a point that we will downplay any negative aspects of ourselves that interfere with our goal of becoming more attractive. This is our flesh in action.

† *Describe the different ways you relate. Share any personal stories.*

THE OLD FLESHLY SELF

As dangerous as the world and Satan are, neither is our greatest problem. Our greatest source of conflict dwells within us, what Paul called "the flesh" or the "old self," also called the enemy of the soul.

Today we call it the "ego." Flippantly, I and a few others call this dark side of ourselves "Flesh Woman."

Literally, flesh is our physical nature, the muscular and fatty tissue parts of the body. Figuratively, flesh is our human nature and humanity's natural orientation away from God. It is equated to our fallen, sinful and dysfunctional nature (Galatians 5:17; Jude 23). The Bible says the moment we are born, the struggle with our flesh begins because we are born slaves to sin (John 8:34).

The flesh represents our natural desires. Desires are good in themselves, such as desires for food, sleep and sex; desires to achieve and succeed. There are proper ways to satisfy each of these desires and there are also divinely imposed limits. This is where Satan strikes. He takes advantage of our bent toward doing precisely what God would not want us to do—like taking credit for blessings God has provided (called pride). James 1:14-15 says,

- *Temptation comes from our own desires* →
- *which entice us and drag us away. These desires* →
- *give birth to sinful actions.* →
- *And when sin is allowed to grow, it gives birth to death.*

When Flesh Woman dominates our lives, we honor all sorts of gods—the god of youth and beauty; the god of money and success; the god of food and sex; as well as celebrities and other super-stars. We get enticed and lured away from Jesus, as James puts it. We make decisions without asking God, then ask Him to bless our decisions. Our thinking is compromised leading to sin. Scripture states,

> *Those who live according to the sinful nature [the flesh] have their minds set on what that nature desires; but those who live in accordance with the Spirit have their minds set on what the Spirit desires (Romans 8:5).*

> *When you follow your own wrong inclinations* (your flesh), *your lives will produce these evil results: impure thoughts, eagerness for lustful pleasure, idolatry, spiritism* (encouraging the activity of demons), *hatred and fighting, jealousy and anger, constant effort to get the best for yourself, complaints and criticisms, the feeling that*

everyone else is wrong except those in your own little group—and there will be wrong doctrine, envy, murder, drunkenness, wild parties, and all that sort of thing (Galatians 5:19-21).

This is important: We are not responsible for the original "flesh womanly" thought when it first pops up. It's what we choose to do with that thought—to act on it or not. If we can simply recognize the ungodly thought, take it captive and give it over to God, then we haven't sinned; we've done good. However, if we do nothing and dwell on the thought, it will eventually stir-up ungodly feelings which leads to ungodly actions, which is sin.

Sin is serious business to God. Our minds have to be changed in such a way that the old values, beliefs and practices are replaced by those which conform to the mind of Christ. The good news is: We are what we are because of who our Parent is. Once this identity becomes deeply rooted in our being, then a new way of thinking and acting becomes a new way of life. We become more others-centered versus Flesh Woman-centered.

TEMPTATION AND IMAGINATION

Known as the "prince of preachers," Charles Spurgeon confessed he wrestled with his imagination,

> Those who have a fair share of imagination know what a difficult thing it is to control. You cannot restrain it. My imagination has taken me down to the vilest kennels and sewers of earth.[40]

Do you identify with Reverend Spurgeon? Neuro-physiologists have discovered that the brain responds to mental images as if the activity were actually happening. There is no difference in the brain wave whether an athlete is swinging a bat or only seeing an image of himself doing so.[41] (Neuro-economists found that imagining a future purchase is almost as good as getting it. Your brain gets a zing whether you purchase or imagine it.[42] So the next time you are tempted to buy those cute black shoes, instead, imagine yourself wearing them. You'll get a zing and save yourself some money.) The same goes for the not-so desirable thoughts.

Paul taught in 2 Corinthians 10:3-5:

For though we walk in the flesh, we do not war according to the flesh (for the weapons of our warfare are not of the flesh, but mighty before God to the casting down of strongholds), casting down imaginations, and every high thing that is exalted against the knowledge of God, and bringing every thought into captivity to the obedience of Christ. (ASV)

Paul mentions three things: *strongholds, imaginations* and a *thought.*
- A thought unchecked →
- Formation of images = imagination →
- Self-image and self-talk

For example, when a thought and/or image says *failure, loser, fat,* that becomes the picture you see of yourself—your self-image—your mindhold.

† *I challenge you to become aware of the images you've created which have become negative mindholds. Which one (or more) comes to your mind right now?*

TENSION BETWEEN FLESH WOMAN AND THE SPIRIT

Have you ever, as they say, stuck your foot in your mouth and said something totally inappropriate, or offended anyone with your humor, antics or jesting? I sure have. When I realized my error, I created in my mind "soul dirt." *Bad me! How could I be so stupid and insensitive? What was I thinking? How humiliating!*

How often is a tormented statement like this on your mind? *"I do not understand what I do. For what I want to do I do not do, but what I hate I do."* Do you find yourself struggling to measure up to the way you think a Christian is supposed to behave? How would you feel if a great Christian leader admitted to a similar struggle? Would you believe the great apostle Paul wrote this (Romans 7:15)? Paul speaks as one caught helplessly between a desire for good and a rebellious will. Many of us know this all too well.

Paul felt the inner tensions between his flesh and the Spirit. Paul the Pharisee was at war with Paul the Christian. His solution was a relationship with God (defined in Romans 8). But his relationship with God didn't completely dissolve the inner tensions. The war still ensued, *but* the nature of the struggle changed.

When the Holy Spirit came to live within Paul, He had a fight on His hands—a fight with the old Paul's ego, the Pharisee. Little does Paul know how normal his condition is. We struggle against forces we really don't understand. I believe Christians often feel uncomfortable admitting to pessimistic thinking or addictive behavior because we mistakenly believe our faith should eliminate all our problems. Not so. The well-known evangelist, D. L. Moody, confessed, "I have had more trouble with myself than with any other man I have ever met!"[43]

The truth is, most of us have a hard time throwing off old habits and self-talk—kicking Flesh Woman off her throne—and relying totally on God. This is because our new self (guided by the Holy Spirit) and our old self (guided by the flesh) are existing side by side. Thus, what we don't want to do we still do—like ruminate, gossip, watch ungodly programming, eat and drink too much, etc. Likewise, what we want to do, like "love our neighbors" and pray and read our Bible for an hour every morning, we just can't seem to make a habit. One part of our mind says to do the better thing, but then we abruptly do the wrong thing.

"WHAT I DON'T WANT TO DO I DO"

Think of the last time you saw a commercial for pizza and then decided you were hungry for a pizza. Research proves that ad campaigns of yummy food directly activate eating-related areas of the brain associated with taste and reward. Food ads, as well as other consumer-oriented ads, act like unconscious behavioral suggestions influencing our consumption—and we're not even aware of their power over us.[44] Even well-intentioned PSAs (*Public Service Announcements*) often have an opposite effect. For example, a stop-smoking campaign contains cues about smoking. Just thinking about quitting smoking activates the same mental pathways and brain networks that are related to the craving for a cigarette. This keeps that unwanted behavior active in the mind—maybe more so than if we were not actively trying not to do it. We can actually become more likely than usual to do exactly what we didn't want to do.

I'm part of a campaign to educate teens and churches to the harms of pornography. Our fear is that by bringing the subject up listeners will want to check it out—which could be completely devastating long-term to that person and ultimately his/her family.

Our attempts at suppressing unwanted behavior work fine as long as we're paying attention to—and actively trying to—suppress the behavior we don't want to do. It's easy when the message is active and accessible in our minds.[45] This is why we desperately need to be close to Jesus each day, so that His presence is working in both our conscious and unconscious minds.

What we think about and which path we walk is a choice we all make each day. Paul gives us this important advice:

> *So, I say, live by the Spirit, and you will not gratify the desires of the* [flesh] *sinful nature. … For the one who sows to his own flesh will from the flesh reap corruption, but the one who sows to the Spirit will from the Spirit reap eternal life" (Galatians 5:16; 6:8).*

Paul recognized the necessity to give his life to Christ daily. He didn't get stuck like many of us have; he chose righteous living. As we separate ourselves from old fleshly thoughts and from toxic products that contaminate our bodies, we find we want to give up the pleasures of the world … and even some old acquaintances. We can have victory over "the desires of the flesh" when we live by God's Holy Spirit.

THE PARADOX

Oscar Wilde once said, "Every saint has a past, and every sinner has a future." "In Christ" I have been set free from the dominion and power of sin (Romans 6:14). When we put our faith in Jesus as our Lord and Savior He breaks every chain and shackle—every stronghold. So why don't I feel free, you may ask? Because I still experience life on earth with a physical body and nature to sin. Flesh Woman still wants to call the shots. Have you ever been to a circus and seen an elephant restrained by a piece of rope to a small wooden stake? This is only possible because the elephant has been held captive since a baby. It will take time to live as a freed slave of the world and our flesh. And it will only be possible if we stay close to Jesus every day.

Does that mean we will never sin again? No. When Paul wrote, *"We died to sin; how can we live in it any longer?" (Romans 6:2),* he was not referring to the act of committing sins, but to continuing to live under the *authority* of sin. There's a difference between the *activity* of sin, which every believer lives with, and the *dominion* of sin, which defines the unbeliever.

While the influence and presence of sin can never be eliminated in this life—*its control can be abolished.* How does this happen? Daily we deny ourselves and submit to God. We take our "soul dirt" to Him and let Him scrub us clean with His grace, mercy and forgiveness.

TEMPTED? PRAY THE LORD'S PRAYER

The first part of 1 Corinthians 10:13 reminds us that dues to our flesh nature, *"No temptation has seized you except what is common to man."* Despite our change in position, we will still be tempted to sin: *"Sin is crouching at the door, eager to control you. But you must subdue it and be its master" (Genesis 4:7).* Consider this illustration:

> Four priests were spending a couple of days at a cabin. In the evening they decided to tell each other their biggest temptation. The first priest said, "It's kind of embarrassing, but my big temptation is looking at skin-revealing pictures. Once I even bought a copy of the *Sports Illustrated Swimsuit Edition.*"
>
> "My temptation is worse," said the second priest. "It's gambling. One Saturday instead of preparing my message I went to the race track to bet on the ponies."
>
> "Mine is worse," said the third priest. "I sometimes can't control the urge to drink. Once I actually broke into the sacramental wine."
>
> The fourth priest was quiet. "Brothers, I hate to say this but my temptation is worst of all. I love to gossip—and if you guys will excuse me, I'd like to make a few phone calls!"

This is an interesting illustration considering in Jesus's day rabbis were quoted, "To which is gossip more similar: robbery or murder? Murder, because robbers can always give you back what they stole; gossips can never repair the damage they've done" (Babylonian Talmud).

If we're going to battle Flesh Woman, we need to pray this sentence of the Lord's prayer: *"And lead us not into temptation, but deliver us from evil"* (Matthew 6:9-13, KJV). When the Hebrews prayed to God to not lead them into temptation, but deliver them from evil, the word *evil (ra)* meant danger or misfortune, as well as sin.

Simply put they prayed, "Deliver me from a bad person, misfortune, an evil inclination, from Satan." Since God doesn't tempt us (James 1:13) it was their way of asking for physical protection.

Jesus basically said, "Don't let us submit to our own evil inclinations. Help us avoid temptation and sin."

✝ *What is God saying to you? What are you going to do about it?*

14 – TORN BETWEEN TWO MASTERS?

Wouldn't you agree that in America, we've come to put our faith in actors, athletes, politicians, musicians, reporters, models and pastors? We see them as larger-than-life figures to be praised and emulated. More disturbing, we see our own lives as somehow inferior. Psychological research by John Maltby and his colleagues found that as the level of religious devotion decreases, which is the trend today, the degree of celebrity worship increases.[46]

When someone has something we desire, we seem to believe we can have the same thing if we imitate that person's behavior. If a person desires power, fame, beauty, wealth or status, they will model their behavior on that of the people they most identify with.

You may remember back in 2010, actor Charlie Sheen received a lot of media attention surrounding excess drinking, drugs, porn stars and trashing hotel rooms. Yet he was the highest paid actor on television for his role on the hit comedy "Two and a Half Men."[47] If I'm a person (especially a teenager) who desires to be a high paid actor, I will likely model his behavior, even if that behavior is reckless and has nothing to do with acting.

French philosopher of social science, Dr. Rene Girard, developed the idea of *mimesis* or *mimetic desires*—a.k.a. *mimicking*. According to Dr. Girard, the *mimetic desire* is motivated by an inner sense that "something" is missing. Scripture says, *"You want something but don't get it" (James 4:2)*. His theory is that our desires never come purely from ourselves; rather, they are inspired by the desires of another.[48] Sociologists and scientists confirm that the more we watch a person or group's behavior, the more we're *unconsciously* motivated to imitate that behavior.

In the age of social media, we are consuming images quicker than ever before—images which lie habitually. Boys learn toughness via males in movies, music videos, and games that present violent masculinity as the cultural norm; girls are starving themselves in order to look like super-models.

In a controversial study, Facebook researchers deliberately manipulated the positivity or negativity of the newsfeed for nearly 700,000 of their users. They found that people made more positive posts if they were exposed to more positive posts by others; people made more negative posts if they were in the group given more negative newsfeeds. Altogether, the research showed that all types of behavior is just as contagious over social networks as in person.

The mimetic desire describes our ravenous hunger for wholeness. Deep inside we feel "something" is missing. It lures many into a dangerous web, creating insatiable consumers of false gods and images. The culture and media machine have done a superb job of getting us to believe "something" is missing and only "more" of what they offer will satisfy … and we devour the bait. Why? Because *lost people are spiritually hungry.*

Bible says, *"When you enter the land the LORD your God is giving you, do not learn to imitate the detestable ways of the nations there"* (Deuteronomy 18:9).

When I got my first beeper, I made sure it was visible for all to see. (Yes, I'm really dating myself.) *Surely, they will think I'm a doctor or some sort of VIP!* I wanted you to think I was a "somebody." Any time we try to be someone else we are in some type of bondage.

As long as you believe you must emulate others, you will never know what you are capable of. There's always someone waiting in the wings to do better than us. Someone will always be prettier or smarter. Their house will be bigger. They will drive a better car. Their children will do better in school. We don't seem to consider that the prettiest woman can be battling depression; the richest person we know may be lonely; the most envied woman at work may be unable to have children.

WHO DO I WORSHIP?

We know Jesus wants to give each one of us an internal makeover which begins with renewing our minds. He knows we'll never find wholeness by imitating other fallen human beings. Jesus said, *"You can't worship two gods at once. Loving one god, you'll end up hating the other. Adoration of one feeds contempt for the other"* (Matthew 6:24, MSG).

As soon as we honestly decide to know and follow Jesus instead of other fallen creatures, the power of our flesh starts diminishing and His grace empowers us. That "something" which was missing is found—Jesus. The apostle Paul tried to imitate Jesus faithfully. He proclaimed, "For *I am not seeking my own good but the good of many, so that they may be saved. Follow my example,* as *I follow the example of Christ"* (1 Corinthians 10:34-11:1).

The concept that God's people must imitate God rather than man is not new. The book of Leviticus repeated some five times the command, *"I am the LORD your God. You must live holy lives. Be holy because I am holy"* (Leviticus 11:44). If we claim to be a Christian to the rest of the world, we are in their eyes expected to be a striking likeness and picture of Jesus Christ. Unfortunately, many who claim to be a Christian are not living a life that imitates Jesus very well. Their minds and lives have not been changed by the indwelling Christ. One well-respected pastor said, "If we Christians are indistinguishable from non-Christians, then we are useless."

† *Might you be "torn between two masters?" Not sure? Pray about it.*

JESUS WITH SKIN ON

The mimicking nature of our mind isn't inherently good or bad—it all depends on the messages and suggestions we receive from the outside world. Our chameleonlike nature makes us more likely to do what other people are presently doing. This means we need to filter out what comes into our minds in order to be more like Jesus.

It sounds like an impossible task—to think like and imitate *the* Jesus Christ. It is unattainable in our own strength. It's only possible through God's grace. God can do immeasurably more than all we ask or imagine. The best artist isn't discouraged. She may not be a Van Gogh—and knows she's not a Van Gogh—but she does her very best to paint a picture of excellence.

Believers are supposed to be "Jesus with skin on." This is one of the ways He makes Himself visible to many who would never pick up a Bible or go to church. Saint Francis of Assisi is known for these famous words, "Preach the gospel every day; if necessary, use words."[49] People are watching the way we act more than they are listening to what we say.

Through studying the Person of Jesus Christ—His work and life example—God gives us what we need to be extraordinary in our particular areas of life. He gives us the Holy Spirit to help us see, think, talk and act more like Jesus. He promises to instruct, counsel and teach us, all the while watching over us (Psalm 32:8).

The purpose of getting to know Jesus intimately is not merely to model His behaviors. *We want to experience Jesus—His love, His touch, His joy—and then release it!* Then we live life freely and fully authentically. I say its time every Christian has "skin in the game"— incurs the risks of "preaching the gospel every day, and if necessary, using words."

✝ ✝ ✝

We are captains of our souls and who doesn't want to be a captain! But—as in any other path of life, there are bad captains and good captains. The wise good captain takes the wind and currents into account, adjusts for when they go against the course, and takes advantage of them when going the same direction. The bad captain insists that only the steering wheel matters, and so crashes into the rocks or ends up adrift at sea.

When we acknowledge and work with our conflict zones, we have a chance to change the direction of our life. Through the power of the Spirit, we regain real control where we never had it before. It was Jimmy Dean who said, "I can't change the direction of the wind, but I can adjust my sails to always reach my destination."

✝ *What do you believe the Spirit is communicating to you at this moment?*

Finally, brothers, whatever is true, whatever is noble, whatever is right, whatever is pure, whatever is lovely, whatever is admirable--if anything is excellent or praiseworthy--think about such things.

–Philippians 4:8

15 — MAN'S FIRST MAJOR DEBACLE

In the fantasy film *Edward Scissorhands,* the character Peg visits a pseudo-medieval mansion on a hill where she finds Edward, a scarred-up creation with scissors for hands. She decides to take him home and adopt him into her family.

In a series of flashbacks, we get a glimpse of Edward's creation process. My heart went out to Edward when his creator died, leaving him an orphan (and without human hands). He always looked so sad and incomplete. I couldn't help but flash to Adam and Eve and think the same. Like Edward, they lost the relationship with their Creator.

Before the fall, Adam and Eve were naked and unashamed (Genesis 2:25). After sinning, they covered themselves, hiding from God. Having lost their source of value and belonging, the couple established insecurity for all of us.

Adam and Eve experienced for the first time *guilt, fear, shame* and *dishonesty.* The first thing they did after disobeying God was to hide from Him. Guilt, in short, is the fear of being found out and punished. We hide when we feel guilty and fearful.

When the couple believed Satan's lies about God, the flow of love and trust broke. The result: selfishness, pride, fear, shame and guilt infected the human heart. Consequently, mankind has distorted, twisted and perverted ideas about God, which has only incited more fear. Genesis 3 concludes with these two life-changing verses,

> *So, the LORD God banished him* [Adam] *from the Garden of Eden to work the ground from which he had been taken. After he drove the man out* [including Eve], *he placed on the east side of the Garden of Eden cherubim and a flaming sword flashing back and forth to guard the way to the tree of life (23-24).*

For the first time, mankind felt *rejection.*

We're going to look at four different emotions in this study that in themselves were created by God to be healthy emotions, but when left unresolved can do damage to our minds, bodies, relationships and spirituality—rejection, fear and worry, anger, shame. (Clearly, there are many other hot emotions we could discuss.)

TAKING OUR EMOTIONS CAPTIVE

When we speak about taking our thoughts captive, this also means taking any toxic emotions captive as well—because every emotion begins with a single thought. This is why describing and naming what we're feeling is vital. God made our emotions and it's important that we experience them fully. It's important to be honest with ourselves and acknowledge our "hot buttons" and insecurities that we're experiencing. And we need to be honest and truthful with God: *I'm afraid! I'm mad as heck! I feel betrayed. I'm full of resentment.*

One woman believed it was dishonoring God by letting her real emotions out. Like the psalmists in the Bible, we can express our heart-felt honest—and very volatile—thoughts and feelings to God. We are all human and all experience negative self-centered thoughts and emotions. The psalmists brought their raw emotions and desires for vindication before God. I encourage you to do the same. God will help you understand your feelings and recognize exactly what you have to take captive and give to Him.

16 — Take Captive Raunchy Rejection

The phone rang. I couldn't believe what I had just heard. In 2009 a producer from the *Focus on the Family Weekend* radio program informed me I'd be one of their featured speakers in the near future. Naturally, I was ecstatic. Then I learned the feature was to be delayed, possibly cancelled, not once, but twice. Was it the devil working in the background or God putting up the obstacles because it wasn't the right time? Perhaps I simply wasn't ready for this kind of exposure.

I finally taped the interview with the host Bill Maher and it ran one Saturday morning on the radio. The segment was released on CD. As I held that little piece of plastic, I beamed with pride. *Praise God! Thank you, Lord!* There's something intoxicating about seeing your name in print and having it known by others. I tasted it for just a moment. When the taped interview wrapped up, Mr. Maher did not mention my book or myself as a resource. *What's wrong with me? Why is my book not good enough to mention like the other Focus on the Family guests?* In that moment, I felt the sting of the worse kind of rejection.

Our world is filled with rejection ("Rejection" can mean *abandonment, refusing to recognize, cast out, discarding as useless, denied* or *renounced*.)—babies aren't wanted, children are abused by their parents, school peers mock and abandon their friends, the disabled are disqualified, parents' divorce, publishers won't publish most manuscripts, or we discover our spouse has chosen someone else (the greatest rejection wound of all). The list goes on. It hurts—big time. This is because God designed us to be loved and accepted.

When we're rejected, we instinctively fight to regain emotional balance. Then we try to find a way to cope via a coping or defense mechanism in order to convince ourselves we haven't been wounded by someone else's rejection. *There's something wrong with them!* We make a vow to our heart, *That's the last time I'll let anyone hurt me like that.* We think we're protecting ourselves, but in reality, we're only trapping ourselves in a pattern of behavior that binds us to bitterness and depression.

The Bible is full of stories about people who were rejected, including Jesus Himself. God was rejected when His top-ranked angel, Lucifer, betrayed Him and left heaven and took with him a cadre of other angels (considered "fallen" angels).

WHY REJECTION HURTS SO MUCH

Think of the last time you felt the sting or pain of being rejected. Rejection just seems to happen; we don't consciously try to figure out why. I'm not a social scientist but I've done quite a bit of research. It appears to me rejection hurts because God created us social beings. He created us to want to spend time with not only Him, but people. They satisfy our need for love and acceptance.

Case in point: Each time your phone rings does a voice inside your head scream, *Yay! Someone needs me. Something needs my attention. I must get to it now!* (If you were to look inside your brain, chances are you'd see a surge of pleasure seeking chemicals.)

Ever bemoan the fact you watch too much TV? Sometimes I do. I say the reason is because I'm either too tired to do anything else, or I'm bored, or there's a "must-see" program. Notice I didn't give you a social reason.

Social scientists say the deeper reason we may watch a lot of TV— or spend hours on social media—is these activities help fill important social needs. That's why things like watching TV and online chatting, or not chatting, is so popular. We feel we are spending time with people, which satisfies our need for social contact.

The point: We are people-oriented; we have a social-self. So, when one of our "peeps" rejects us, it wounds because a need we are seeking to be filled is not filled—in fact it may be filled with poison.

✝ Share a personal story when your need to satisfy your social-self was not met by someone important to you.

REJECTION FOR OUR BENEFIT?

God designed rejection for our benefit.

Like you, I was taken back when Bob Sorge stated in his book *Dealing with the Rejection and Praise of Man*. For our benefit? Is this guy nuts? As I read on, the more sense it made. Let me share with you what he taught me.[50]

Pastor Sorge asserts that a substantial step towards our freedom is made when we're able to see God as the author of life's rejections and not men. Although men give out rejection, God ultimately allows it in His sovereign plan for a divine purpose. The sting of rejection that we feel, unbeknownst to us, is accomplishing something very profound in our soul and spirit. If we respond properly, the rejection will be used by God to shape and conform us into the image of Christ. He wrote, "Properly embraced, rejection can become a gift."

Think about it: Those God uses the most are always rejected the most like Jesus, David, the prophets, the apostles and many others. It appears it's an essential element in God's process of shaping our characters. It appears to be a vital ingredient in the training up of leaders and a necessary tool to teach us humility.

None of us wants to be rejected. I know when I am, then I don't feel affirmed. And when I don't feel affirmed I can feel stupid, or misunderstood, or unloved, or that I don't belong. The point is: That's exactly how Jesus felt. Yet, even though He was pained by rejection, His soul and spirit were never wounded by it. He never embraced bitterness or felt offended by it. *He found a way to process rejection so it stung Him without wounding Him.*

When we view rejection as a "gift" from God to keep our hearts pliable, humble and dependent on Him, we gain a new freedom from man's rejection. John Knox wrote, "One man with God on his side is always a majority." So, prepare yourself: You'll never grow beyond the need for rejection to tenderize your heart before God. *Embrace rejection as an opportunity for your character development.*

GOD'S HEALING BALM

No question rejection hurts—a lot. Thankfully God provides a healing balm for these wounds—His amazing unconditional love. He loves and accepts you, warts and all, even when you blow it. God loves you so much that He gave His one and only Son—the same Son who so desperately loves you too (John 3:16).

By knowing that God loves us and will not reject us, we can come to "love our neighbor" regardless of how he/she treats us. Proverbs 29:25 states, *"The fear of human opinion disables; trusting in God protects you from that" (MSG).*

When genuine Love and Truth pours into our lives and minds, not only does fear, guilt and shame decrease, but growth, character development and healthy thinking improves. When we worship *the real God—our brains, characters and lives are changed.* The neural circuitry in our brains is changed positively.

But be aware: Your enemy, the devil, will do *anything* to hinder you from accepting and receiving this love. Don't doubt God's love—ever. Believe this good news and be set free from the rejection and wounds of your past.

† *Now that you've taken in what most likely is a brand-new perspective on the topic of rejection, describe how this makes you feel. How willing are you to accept this gift from God?*

THE SNARE OF PRAISE

Do you realize that rejection and praise are at the opposite ends of the same continuum but with *identical roots?* Pastor Sorge said, "Those who fear the rejection of man have a deep yearning for the praise of man and set their souls up for repetitive heartache."[51]

I never felt attractive or that I belonged growing up. Every time my family moved (five times before I started college) I seemed destined to meet Raunchy Rejection. My classmates nicknamed me Bozo, after the clown. Consequently, I had an insatiable appetite for love and acceptance. I believed that if I were "perfect" then I'd get all the affirmations I needed to be happy. I chased after worldly riches, successes and acceptance just to dull the pain (which is where my addiction to food, body image and alcohol came in). It was too hard to keep the Cover Girl mask on each day.

It's been said for every one positive comment made, a child receives 10 negative comments; and it takes 7 compliments to undo the effects of just one criticism. No wonder we grow up feeling we need to do whatever it takes to be accepted. We thrive on praise.

Often called "the rejection syndrome," many of us find ourselves basing our self-worth on how others see us and our accomplishments. We live a life we cannot sustain because we unknowingly have bought into the lies and accusations. This is a giant mindhold. We often call these people "people-pleasers" and "perfectionists." They think: *I must be loved or approved by every significant person in my life. I depend on others for my value; I must be competent and perfect in order to receive praise and thereby consider myself worthwhile.*

If we're living to make sure others like us, we give them the power to determine our self-worth. I must constantly remind myself I work for God, not people. I can't allow other people's approval or disapproval of me dominate my thinking. That's a mindhold. We're *all* wired to be mistake makers. That's why pencils have erasers! Two pastors at my church said, "Mistakes have shaped me—but they're not who I am."

The Bible is clear: we're not to actively seek out the praise of man (John 5:44). In the Old Testament King Saul obeyed the people instead of God because he feared people more than God, which God considered a great insult (1 Samuel 15:24). This is another one of those counter-cultural teachings. Flesh Woman desires to be noticed and seen. God desires we first receive affirmation from Him (Acts 5:29; Galatians 1:10).

There are two reasons why we're cautioned against seeking man's admiration:

1. *People are fickle.* One minute they love you, the next they turn their back to you. Even Christians eventually disappoint.

2. *What other people think really doesn't matter in the grand scheme of eternity.* When we stand before God at the end of our lives, other people's opinions won't matter a bit. Only God's opinion will be relevant (2 Corinthians 10:18).

God's own Son Jesus stated, *"I do not accept praise from men"* (John 5:41). The only honor Jesus received was from the Father: *"This is my Son, whom I love; with him I am well pleased"* (Matthew 3:17). How then do we receive praise and accolades from the Father? Let me suggest:

1—*Let Him speak to you through His Word* as you study the Bible. God speaks to and affirms us repeatedly. Second Timothy 3:16 tells us, *"the whole Bible was given to us by inspiration from God and is useful to* **teach us what is true** *..."*

2—*Pray and listen* for His quiet voice to speak into your mind.

3—*Discern proper praise from other people.* God created us to need encouragement from each other. The Bible tells us we are to build one another up daily (Hebrews 3:13; Romans 14:19; 1 Thess. 3:2). In this society we tend to over-praise each other. When Jesus affirmed His disciples, He didn't gush all over them to keep them propped up emotionally. When He praised them, it was very strategic: He affirmed what God was doing through them.

Pastor Sorge wrote, "I do not seek the praise of other people, but I do seek to honor and encourage other believers as much as possible."[52] Praise that encourages and builds us up in the body of

Christ is biblical (1 Thess. 5:11). Sam Walton, founder of Wal-Mart said, "Nothing else can quite substitute for a few well-chosen, well-timed, sincere words of praise. They're absolutely free and worth a fortune."[53] Try to catch your kids, or employees, or spouse doing something "praiseworthy" as Philippians 4:8 puts it, and tell them so.

✝ ✝ ✝

The goal of spiritual growth is not perfection but maturity. Our growth in Jesus will bear fruit in a transformed life and character (see Galatians 5:22–23). But we will still have issues and struggles.

Paul said, *"Not that I have already obtained all this, or have already arrived at my goal, but I press on to take hold of that for which Christ Jesus took hold of me" (Philippians 3:12).* We must press on and not let our imperfections get us down.

✝ *Finish each sentence:*

- When people compliment me, I feel …
- I feed off other people's praise because …
- Seeking God's praise instead of another's feels to me like …

17 — Take Captive Fatal Fear and Wicked Worry

Fear is not real. The only place that fear can exist is in our thoughts of the future. It is a product of our imagination, causing us to fear things that do not at present, and may not, ever exist. Do not misunderstand me, danger is very real, but *fear is a choice.* We are all telling ourselves a story and that day mine changed.[54]

This quote is from the movie *After Earth* spoken by Will Smith about toxic and fatal fear. It's been said that "fear" stands for: *False Evidence Appearing Real*. It's based on our thoughts and feelings about events that may or *may not* ever happen. Have you noticed toxic fear always seems to find a comfortable hiding place in our minds?

There are two kinds of fear. *Positive fear* which is God-given and toxic *negative fear* which is from Satan and is destructive.

POSITIVE FEAR

Positive fear keeps you alive. It motivates you to buy home insurance (fear of fire), to follow the law (fear of prison), or to obey (fear of discipline). It can be a powerful ally in the face of danger when your "gut" says to play dead, or to stop breathing, or to run and scream or fight, or just be quiet. This kind of positive fear can help us predict violent behavior. (Note: Being cautious is constructive but *remaining in a state if fear is destructive*. Anxiety disorders develop when normal fear becomes pathological.)

We also "fear" God (Proverbs 1:7). When the Bible says to fear the Lord, it doesn't mean we're afraid of Him, like He's some kind of tyrant. It means we hold Him up in reverence with respect and in awe. Scripture says, *"God is greatly feared; he is more awesome than all who surround him"* (Psalm 89:7).

Love is what we are born with. *Fear is what we learn.*

- For **God has not given us a spirit of fear**, *but of power and of love and of a sound mind (2 Timothy 1:7).*
- *With his love, he will calm all your fears. … There is no fear in love. But* **perfect love drives out fear**, *because fear has to do with punishment. (Zephaniah 3:17; 1 John 4:18).*

God's love is not coercive and that *love has the power to cast out fear*—but this also means that fatal *fear has the power to cast out love*. Where love is absent, fear sets in. When we are not loved unconditionally, then we believe we aren't good enough, and we lose power. Instead, negative fear sets. It squashes learning, warps and stunts us, makes us addicted and neurotic.

Negative Fear

Our greatest crises come from the kind of fear that tells us we won't be able to handle something. We're afraid of failing; of being alone or rejected; of running out of money; feeling the pain of the past; that someone will let us down; afraid we won't find a husband or a job, or we will be assaulted or conned; afraid that if we let ourselves be sad for our losses that we'll never be able to stop crying.

Try this: If you fear something, then look up statistical odds of that happening (the probability is undoubtedly low).

Studies confirm that people who focus on negative aspects of themselves, or of life, generate waves of fear which release a flood of destructive neurochemicals into the brain.[55] Our bodies release the hormone *cortisol* which weakens the immune system, kills brain cells and causes weight gain. ☺

When you live in a constant state of anxiety or fear, you live in bondage and oppression because you are physically, emotionally, relationally and spiritually unable to focus on anything else. You lose all ability to concentrate and are unable to ingest truth. The truth about fear is it is rooted in the belief that God's Word won't work. If we are fear-driven and believe, for example, "I'm not worthy of love," or "God is against me," or "Others are trying to hurt and control me," then our behavior will match our perceived thinking.

There is one last kind of fear I want to address: *Fear of letting ourselves be known*. Because of less than favorable past experiences, many of us can't—or won't—let others access certain parts of ourselves. People, like actors, try to create a favorable impression. There are "front stage" public personas or facades; there are "backstage" private personas. Exposing ourselves is scary. When you feel safe and you're with people you trust, you'll unlock the door, and the fear will gradually dissipate.

I challenge you to identify the front stage facade that you've created in order to cover the fear-based backstage feelings. We hold the key—Jesus— who opens the locked doors.

WICKED WORRY

Fear is not the same as worry but they're close cousins. Someone said *worry is fear that we manufacture—of an imaginary future—which tends not to exist.* The word comes from an old English word that means "to strangle or choke." When we worry, we're strangling or choking our emotions and blocking any flow of creative energy in our lives. So, we must choose to learn to live in the present moment.

Jesus said, *"Therefore do not worry about tomorrow, for tomorrow will worry about itself. Each day has enough trouble of its own"* (Matthew 6:34). He's saying that nothing should cause us to fear or worry.

Think about this: Every day we traverse through a dangerous world. You and I have survived some extraordinary feats considering we move around in and through powerful machines that could kill us: cars, airplanes, buses, trains, escalators, elevators. We're surrounded by toxic chemicals in our workplace, home and in our foods. Our homes are hooked up to explosive gases and lethal currents of electricity. We live among evil and hateful people. Put together, we could live with worry and dreaded fear. Instead, we should be amazed and thank God that we've survived.

Have faith: God has, and will continue to, protect us. Faith is the one power which fear and worry cannot stand on. We can handle anything—good or bad—that comes our way.

TRY THIS "OBLITERATE WORRY" EXERCISE

A reputable study stated *only 8 %* of what we worry about in the future ever comes true, or that 92 % of what we worry about *won't* come true. List numerically on a piece of paper every situation you're presently worried about. When finished, take 8 % of that number.

For example, if you list 15 worries; 15 X 8 % = 1.2 of your worries will come true. The mind of Christ counteracts the number by remembering that if something troublesome does happen, God will use it for good (Romans 8:28; Genesis 50:20). We can come into God's presence and experience "the peace which surpasses all understanding" (Philippians 4:7).

Please don't obsess over which worry is going to come true!

† † †

Brené Brown wrote, "Faith is a place of mystery, where we find the courage to believe in what we cannot see and the strength to let go of our fear of uncertainty."

There is no area in your life that God's *love* cannot enable you to break down mindholds of fear or worry. The truth is: God is love which means Love is within us. That Love will drive away fear. Our journey with God is the relinquishment of fear and the acceptance of faith and Love into our minds and hearts.

God said, *"I have set before you life and death, blessings and curses. Now choose life … (Deuteronomy 30:19).* Fear paralyzes and causes death. God says to choose life and put that fear behind us. If we don't, it will only master our lives.

Day by day, as we fill our minds with God's truth, there will be no room for fear. God says, *"Fear not … you are mine"* (Isaiah 43:1). Instead of asking the fear-based question, "How might I be hurt or die?" we ask, "How can I live?" You can break the hold of these mindholds. Faith shouts back to Satan, "I am not going to fear or worry because I'm God's daughter!" Don't let fear or worry define you. Drink from Jesus's fountain of life!

† *Ask yourself:*
- *What does God mean when He speaks of fear?*
- *What is God saying to me?*
- *What am I going to do about it?*

18 — Take Captive Awry Anger

One evening a husband declared to his wife, "Perhaps you should start washing your clothes in *Slim Fast*. Maybe it would take a few inches off your rear-end!" His wife was hurt and mad. So, she sought revenge. The next morning the husband took a pair of underwear out of his drawer. A little dust cloud appeared. So, he asked her, "Why did you put baby powder in my underwear?" She snickered, "It's not baby powder ... it's *Miracle Grow.*" Then he got really angry!

We don't know if he ever got back at her, or if they played a game of "musical revenge." (I cannot confirm this is a true story.)

It's normal to feel justified to want to hurt the person who hurt us—*what goes around comes around* we rationalize. Many feel their anger is justified. They bring into the present past injustices, bitterness and resentments. Be aware: Justifiable anger can make us feel we are *entitled* to our feelings and reactions, therefore, that "chip on the shoulder" is much harder to let go of.

Some women choose to hide the anger and rage because they don't want to meet with rejection and disapproval; others don't want to show the pain. Some women create a high level of chaos and violence which tells me they've been violated, betrayed and are in a lot of pain.

Have you noticed anger has a cumulative effect? If something or someone makes you mad and you don't deal with it, then when something else makes you mad, you react doubly angry because the anger only builds up inside more and more. Old anger lingers, and the anger we experienced 5 minutes ago can unconsciously trigger all the old antagonistic experiences.

Anger and revenge are classic coping mechanisms, and symptoms of trauma and loss and rejection. It feels safer to show anger than to show our wounds of fear, pain, confusion, terror, shame and grief. And the thing with anger is, we feel sure we are right.

HEALTHY ANGER

Anger is a God-given emotion; a natural and appropriate response to oppression and wrongdoing; to broken trust and unfaithfulness. It's a normal healthy response when our basic needs aren't met (especially when we're children), or when our rights have been violated and to any perceived threat. Anger is healthy when expressed with the intention of informing others about our personal limits, values, rules and boundaries. Aristotle once said,

> Anyone can become angry—that is easy. But to be angry with the right person, to the right degree, at the right time, for the right purpose, and in the right way—this is not easy.

Anger is a very seductive emotion; its profoundly energizing and exhilarating. It is God's response too. God is love, but there are things that make Him angry. There are things He even hates. Proverbs 6:16 states, *"For there are six things the Lord hates—no, seven: haughtiness, lying, murdering, plotting evil, eagerness to do wrong, a false witness, sowing discord among brothers."* God gets angry at injustice and *"evil men who push away the truth" (Romans 1:18).*

Jesus Christ became angry when people were victimized; when God's will was thwarted; when God was misrepresented. This is justifiable anger. Like any parent, God gets angry at His kids. He gives us boundaries and rules because He loves us and wants to protect us from the consequences of sin. When we break those boundaries, His justified anger is reflecting His love for us.

✝ *The next time you get angry, ask yourself if your anger is righteous or selfish. We will come to know what those righteous issues are as we study the Bible.*

UNDERLYING EMOTIONS

Quite frequently, our anger, or passive aggressiveness, is a mask for other painful feelings (without actually speaking our thoughts). Anger has many "teeth" to it. For example, when we've been humiliated, violated, betrayed; or when we're jealous, critical, frustrated, we act angry. Often, we have buried grief, which comes out as anger.

For example: Say your husband or boyfriend says something, either intentionally or unintentionally, that makes you feel degraded and humiliated. Rather than sharing your hurt feelings with him, in an act of self-protection, you may automatically and unconsciously react by finding something to attack him for. It may be something petty or an act of revenge. You're basically attempting to make him feel the same way you feel—demeaned and hurt, "You're the one who is more bad!" Now you don't feel as shamed and hurt—at least temporarily.

When intentions for our lives don't turn out as we desire, we get angry and fail to recognize that we are sad over our losses. The solution is to reframe the anger as sadness and mourn those losses. If we don't, unresolved anger gives the enemy an entry point into our lives. A *feeling chart* can help us dig down to discover what we're really feeling and trying to say.

TRANSFORMING PASSIVE/AGGRESSIVE ANGER

There once lived a very angry racist. He joined lynch mobs for sport. He dedicated his life to hunting down and murdering his enemies. Then something radical happened to this hostile human. God transformed him into a "new creation" (2 Corinthians 5:17).

I'm speaking of the great apostle Paul. Paul met Jesus in a supernatural experience which changed his life forever. He went on to teach the gospel of Christ to the first century world, which was quite a feat considering there was no "Christianity" religion at the time. This is not to say Paul's transformation was a magical once-for-a-lifetime event. He had to unlearn his old thinking patterns and habits of hostility and learn new Christlike thinking. He had to be constantly in the process of taking off his old self and putting on his new self—Jesus. Paul was the one who said of *all* Christians, *"We have the mind of Christ" (1 Corinthians 2:16)*. This means you have the ability to transform your anger—and any other toxic feeling—into Christlike thinking.

Ephesians 4:26-27 says: *"Don't sin by letting anger control you. Don't let the sun go down while you are still angry, for anger gives a foothold to the devil."* Satan knows betrayal, bitterness and anger are destructive. It's a popular poison he uses. Like cancer, anger feelings contaminate our lives by corroding the soul and disorganizing our thinking.

Scientists say that if we allow anger to dominate our thinking, we lose the neurological ability to act compassionately and think logically.[56] It increases the risk of cardiovascular disease and other health problems. Therefore, we must decide to resolve it. Ask God to help you answer, *"What is the issue or pain behind my anger? How shall I work through my anger righteously?"*

Many professionals suggest "blow off steam" by, for example, whacking a punching bag or attacking a pillow or yelling at a stuffed doll. Yet, research has shown this type of therapy does not make people less angry. It actually feeds the flame, making them more angry and aggressive.[57]

What's the solution? Scripture states: *"Fools vent their anger, but the wise quietly hold it back" (Proverbs 29:11);* *"... get rid of anger, rage, malicious behavior ...." (Colossians 3:8).*

Brain expert, Dr. Norman Doidge, suggests *doing something satisfying and fulfilling* when the feeling of anger strikes. A new brain circuit forms that gradually takes precedence over the anger circuit (or any toxic emotion). By *not* acting on the anger, the old anger circuit is weakened—so is the accompanying anxiety and toxic thinking. Contrarily, locking into anger by for example punching a pillow, only locks in and strengthens that brain circuit making it more difficult to get out of—in addition to the continual pouring out of toxins which circulate throughout the body.

Many professionals suggest writing an "anger letter" which may or may not be sent. Since anger is most often disguised as grief, I suggest writing a "grief letter" instead. In a grief letter, we're not likely to express our feelings aggressively, thereby making us angrier. We speak about the losses we feel we've had to bear. We're actually weakening the anger circuit in the brain. An honest grief letter can express deep (anger) emotions which help to close unresolved issues.

Write whatever your heart is aching to say. If the person has died, saying good bye completes the communication. This letter is not intended to be sent. It's intended only to be read to God and another person or group. It can give us a sense of closure. Then what we find is our angry feelings subside.

Depending on the circumstances, coming to *forgive* the person who caused you pain and sadness, may be a substantial leg of your healing journey. By not forgiving, it allows the offending person to control our life—no matter where they live, even if they are dead. This is why an upcoming chapter is devoted to the subject.

ANGER STYLES

Passive   Aggressive

Assertive anger is expressed through direct communication.

Assertive style of anger is often considered the healthy way to express anger. Assertive anger directed to an individual is conveyed in the most responsible manner through assertive communication. In this type of anger, aggression or uncontrolled bursts of emotions do not come into the picture. Then there is no damage to the relationship because the person communicates properly the reason behind her anger, and is ready to take full responsibility if she has hurt someone else.

† *If you are struggling with anger, which do you believe is your anger style. Define it and then talk about why you believe it is your style. Give some examples.*

†††

Let me wrap up by saying that if you find that your anger is too strong to control; if you scare the people in your life; if your anger ever causes you to become physical with the person at whom you are angry, or anyone else who happens to be in the wrong place at the wrong time when you explode—please *get professional faith-based help.*

19 — TAKE CAPTIVE SEPTIC SHAME

My senior year in college was ending. The junior class had a tradition of "roasting" (means to *humorously* mock or humiliate the person with jokes or dissing) the senior class with a "special gift." Most girls knew I was bulimic and addicted to laxatives, so I feared what toxic tribute waited for me. My gift was a box of laxatives. Mortified, my face turned scarlet red. Even though I wanted to run and cry, I laughed with the rest of them. You might as well have embedded a scarlet "S" for "shame-filled" on my forehead. Their gesture only strengthened the erroneous core belief I was irreparably flawed. As I anxiously sat through rest of the roasting I prayed another girl would be crucified, since misery loves company. No such luck. I died alone; mortified.

With shame, everybody else is in on the "the joke" except the person who is going through it. *Shame is real pain.* It's the intensely painful feeling that we are unworthy of love and belonging. It's the most primitive human emotion *we all feel*—and the one no one wants to talk about. *You've most likely been plagued by it most of your life and never identified it as shame.* (The only people who don't experience shame are those who lack a conscience and the capacity for empathy and human connection.) I believe shame is the most toxic human emotion. Think about this: If we didn't long to be wanted and loved, then we wouldn't care. If we didn't care, then we couldn't be shamed by other's rejection or attacks.

We're not the only ones who have carried the burden of shame— Jesus felt it as He hung completely naked and despised on the cross. In fact, in His day, humiliating and shaming someone in public was considered to be like murder because "the pain of humiliation is more bitter than death." The rabbis called this a sin, a "whitening of the face" because a person "pales with shame." They said "one should rather fling himself into a fiery furnace than shame someone in public" (Babylonian Talmud). The rabbis knew the great damage one sharp retort could do.

THE LIE YOU BELIEVED ABOUT YOURSELF

Shame comes out of a lie someone told you about yourself—a lie that you were 'less than.' It may have been a silent lie. For example, if your mom gave you the silent treatment when you did something she considered bad or wrong. The point is: These were lies told to you. They're not yours to replay and relive! I say fling those lies into the fiery furnace!

Shame becomes an obstacle to believing we're capable of changing because *we believe our shameful thoughts are true.* Consider how your life would look different if you no longer evaluated yourself—your worthiness—by the lie someone told you about yourself.

† *Complete these two exercises:*

1. *List 3 things you fear your family and friends might say about you if they were asked to "roast" you at a party.*
2. *Finish this sentence: "If my feelings of shame and guilt could talk, they'd say ..."*

STEP ONE: NAME IT AND SPEAK IT

Shame expert Dr. Brené Brown believes that if we cultivate enough awareness about shame to *name it and speak it*, we can cut it off at the knees. She wrote, "Shame hates having words wrapped around it. If we speak shame, it begins to wither ... language and story bring light to shame and destroy it."[58]

Dr. Brown advocates that the *courage to be vulnerable* means taking off the armor we use to protect ourselves, putting down the weapons that we use to keep people at a distance, showing up and letting ourselves be seen without fear of feeling "naked."[59]

Shame is tough to talk about. But bringing it out into the light isn't nearly as toxic as remaining silent. Then the devil wins. What he doesn't tell you is *everyone* experiences shame and we're all afraid to talk about it—but when we do talk about it, the less control it will have over our lives.

Research proves that when we don't discuss a traumatic event, such as our shame-based experiences, it can be more damaging than the actual event. Conversely, when people shared their feelings, their mental and physical health improved.

† *What does this kind of vulnerability feel like to you?*

STEP TWO: CLARIFY OWNERSHIP

Miranda described an incident with her husband, Joe, in which he told her dinner must be ready at exactly 6:00 PM. Miranda served dinner at 6:10 PM. This did not please Joe. To strike back, he threw his plate into the sink, breaking it. With fire in his eyes, he proceeded to give Miranda the silent treatment for rest of the night. The next morning, shaking his head and pointing his index finger straight into her face, Joe stated, "Why do *you* disrespect my wishes? I wouldn't have to punish you if you'd serve dinner when I ask you to."

Typical of *battered woman's syndrome* Miranda responded, "It wasn't his fault. It's mine. I'm a bad wife, totally inadequate."

To free ourselves from shame, we need to figure out who is responsible. We *clarify ownership*. Let's analyze this situation. Miranda had surrendered her identity to her husband and accepted his version of reality as her own. It's clear that it is the *result of Joe's actions and words* that created Miranda's shame. Consider what Jesus said:

> *The things that come out of the mouth come from the heart, and these make a man 'unclean.' For out of the heart come evil thoughts, murder, adultery, sexual immorality, theft, false testimony, slander. These are what make a man 'unclean' …* (Matthew 15:18-20).

> *The good man brings good things out of the good stored up in his heart, and the evil man brings evil things out of the evil stored up in his heart. For out of the overflow of his heart his mouth speaks* (Luke 6:45).

"EMPATHY EROSION"

Dr. Simon Baron-Cohen, a researcher and expert on the emotion of empathy, doesn't like the term "evil" and prefers to call human cruelty "empathy erosion."[60] *Empathy* essentially is when we identify with what another person is thinking or feeling, and then respond to them with an appropriate emotion. The risk to the person who comes into contact with a person with empathy erosion is being on the receiving end of verbal assaults, physical attacks, or experiencing a lack of care or consideration.[61]

There is a small percent of the population who lack any empathy (zero empathy) because they have a personality disorder (narcissist, borderline, psychopath). Dr. Baron-Cohen believes there are degrees of underactivity in the empathy circuit in these brains. Usually, beliefs drive cruel behavior with most of the unempathetic population. But their empathy circuitry may be misfiring. To overcome, God and professional therapy is required.

JESUS'S WORDS ABOUT UNCLEANLINESS

Some people torment us into believing we're dirty, unworthy and unacceptable to God and to others and we're to blame. In biblical times, this condition was called "unclean." Unclean translated means "impure." Impurities—emotional or chemical—pollute the system and desecrate God's temple, which is us.

In this Scripture Jesus is saying: *It's not what goes in my mouth that defiles me; it's what comes out of my mouth and heart that defiles me.* The mouth reveals most clearly the condition of the heart and thereby behavior. Therefore, if another person spews their verbal vomit onto me—calls me a *blah … blah … blah*, they cannot destroy my soul with their tongue, or make me feel contaminated because the verbal vomit came out of *their* mouth; it came out of *their* heart.

Jesus said, *"Don't be afraid of those who want to kill your body; they cannot touch your soul" (Matthew 10:28).* The only thing that can dirty me is what comes from inside of my heart. When we love another person, and that person has power and authority over us, we tend to take the person's "unclean" dirty words and internalize them; believe they are truth. This is what Miranda did. We believe the lies and convince ourselves we're defiled and condemn ourselves. This is how people maintain power and control over us. The fact is: Joe is the unclean person, not Miranda. He is the *only* person at fault.

† *Explain in your own words what Jesus's therapeutic words of wisdom taught you. What does "clean" mean to you?*

INVESTIGATE THE TRUTH: ALREADY CLEAN

Decades ago when my dad called me a "fat piggy" I internalized and believed it. Healing meant investigating this statement. *Was it true?* I believed it was. I saw fat in the mirror. *Could I be absolutely certain it was true?* Upon further investigation, I recognized I was a little overweight, but I'd never been a "fat piggy." I was "clean." Dad's critical labels made him unclean—not anything I did or ate. *Other people's evil words only taint themselves and make them filthy.* Jesus said,

> *You are already clean because of the word I have spoken to you. Remain in me, as I also remain in you. No branch can bear fruit by itself; it must remain in the vine. Neither can you bear fruit unless you remain in me.*

(In biblical times agriculture was the people's mainstay which is why Jesus and others used gardening and farming illustrations so often.)

What a beautiful description of *your* personal relationship with Christ! You connecting with Jesus; He connecting with you. Let's break this down. To "remain" or "abide" in Jesus is to be rooted and grounded and filled with Him. The result: We are part of Him. We are one. We are clean.

What is your response? Do you really believe what Jesus says is truth? If yes, then *you* are "clean." Remain connected to Jesus and you'll continue to be clean and pure—free from any kind of contamination.

In this parable, we are the branch—the branch attached to Jesus, the vine. According to *Vines Complete Expository Dictionary*, the word "fruit" means "the visible expression of Christ's power working inwardly and invisibly" inside of me. So, let's read it again in this context: *To receive the visible expression of Christ's power working inwardly and invisibly in you; you must remain in Jesus Christ.*

That is to say, when I connect with Christ, His power will be at work in me. I will produce good stuff, not bad stuff. In biblical terms, I'm a "good tree." Jesus said, *"A good tree cannot bear bad fruit, and a bad tree cannot bear good fruit"* (Matthew 7:18).

- Fact: You are connected to Jesus.
- Fact: You are clean.
- Fact: You are the image of "good fruit" and a "good tree;" of goodness, not sin!

Let this sink in: Even if you've had contact with an unclean person, as a believer in Jesus Christ and His Word, *you cannot bear bad or evil things!* Grasping the truth of Jesus's words doesn't change what happened, but it does change our perceptions of the event; it doesn't rewrite the past, but it does rewire the brain by rewriting a shame-based sense of self. It's kind of like the crucifixion and the resurrection. The crucifixion represents the shame and fear; the resurrection is the reverse—a shift in thought from shame and fear to loving ourselves.

Let me conclude this teaching with another Jesus truth. He said, *"... on the day of judgment people will give an account for every careless word they speak ... (Matthew 12:36).*

† *Jesus has a lot to say. This is a lot of good news to take in and digest. I suggest you meditate and hold your thoughts for at least 12 minutes on one or two of these Scriptures each day for the next two weeks. Ponder what God's Word is teaching you about yourself and your feelings of shame.*

SHAME WHICH COMES FROM OUR ACTIONS

To cope with anxiety, pain or trauma, it is not unusual to:

- Act out the pain in a destructive manner, and thereby, hurt ourselves and others.
- Become sharp-tongued, rude or abusive.

- Choose illegal or addictive behaviors in order to cope, such as shoplifting, drug abuse or compulsive behaviors.

Shame is not only a product of what others have done to you, it's also a product of what you've done to yourself and others. Guilt and shame can come as a result of breaking God's laws.

What we learn about Jesus in the Bible is that He reinforced the idea that people should take responsibility for their own actions and lives. He never told people to go to God with other people's problems or offenses (Luke 6:41). We go to God with our own baggage; confess our wrongdoings and ask for His forgiveness, which He grants immediately.

BATYA

Throughout the Bible, we read stories of people who lives were defined by a problem, a label. In the book of John there is a story of a woman who, filled with shame, was brought before Jesus as a condemned woman caught in the act of adultery.

> *Early the next morning he was back again at the Temple. A crowd soon gathered, and he sat down and taught them. As he was speaking, the teachers of religious law and the Pharisees brought a woman who had been caught in the act of adultery. They put her in front of the crowd. "Teacher," they said to Jesus, "this woman was caught in the act of adultery. The law of Moses says to stone her. What do you say?" They were trying to trap him into saying something they could use against him, but Jesus stooped down and wrote in the dust with his finger. They kept demanding an answer, so he stood up again and said, "All right, but let the one who has never sinned throw the first stone!" Then he stooped down again and wrote in the dust. When the accusers heard this, they slipped away one by one, beginning with the oldest, until only Jesus was left in the middle of the crowd with the woman. Then Jesus stood up again and said to the woman, "Where are your accusers? Didn't even one of them condemn you?" "No, Lord," she said. And Jesus said, "Neither do I. Go and sin no more."*

This woman is merely identified as "the adulteress woman." Soren Kierkegaard said, "When you label me, you negate me." Let's not negate this precious lady with the "adulteress" label. Let's call her *Batya* which means "daughter of God."[62]

Most likely trembling with fear, Batya looked into the face of her Judge. Unlike the other men, Jesus looked at her—not her breasts, nor her shame. He saw her differently. His love, kindness and grace pierced through the shame. Immediately, Batya felt a warmth and peace like nothing she'd ever felt before. When Jesus looked into the eyes of Batya, in essence He said,

"My precious daughter, your past is not your present. Don't give in to that masked woman who betrays you. You can say no. Stand up for yourself. You're made in my image! You have immense value. Stop seeing yourself as an adulteress and see yourself as my daughter. I forgive you; now forgive yourself. Now go and stay pure."

No condemnation. No mention of uncleanliness. No anger. Just affirmation, validation, and good news. He purified her. If Batya was unaware of being loved and valued at the beginning of the story, she certainly felt it by the end. Jesus wanted the crowd to know that she was healed and restored as a full member of their community.

Jesus cares. And He can heal you too.

✝ ✝ ✝

What I love about Jesus is He constantly associated with people who were considered "bad" or "unclean" by others, like tax collectors, prostitutes—sinners. But He never thought of them as "bad." He condemned the sinful behavior, but never the sinner. To Jesus, every person had the ability to turn their lives around (repent) and have a relationship with the Father. He constantly invited other people into a relationship with Him because He knew *connecting with Him* is what gave them the power to be who He created them to be.

The Bible states,

Anyone who belongs to Christ has become a new person. The old life is gone; a new life has begun! ... For God made Christ, who never sinned, to be the offering for our sin, so that we could be made right with God through Christ (2 Cor. 5:17; 21) ... For we are God's masterpiece. He has created us anew in Christ Jesus, so we can do the things he planned for us long ago (Ephesians 2:10).

Never forget that when we accept Christ as Lord, the Bible tells us there is a supernatural exchange: *our sin for His righteousness; our shame for His purity.* We are created "anew"—recreated to think and act differently—like Christ. Shame exterminated!

† BALLOON EXERCISE

Your sense of shame all started with one lie you were told about yourself. Name that lie. One of the interactive exercises I do is give each woman a balloon and marker. First, she blows up the balloon and then draws her face on it. Then I ask each woman to stand up and recall the biggest shame-based lie she has believed and to share it with God. Then I say: "On the count of three, sit down and bust the balloon—*bust the lie.* 1-2-3! Satan's domain over this lie has now been broken!" Then rejoice and celebrate!

Warning: If you do this in a church or retreat center, warn the person in charge. The first time I did this, a manager rushed into the room thinking he heard gun shots! If doing this is not possible, take out a piece of paper and write your lie on it. Then tell Satan his domain over this lie will now be broken and destroy the paper!

G.R.O.W.
[God Restores Our Worth]

Don't let others spoil your faith and joy with their philosophies, their wrong and shallow answers built on men's thoughts and ideas, instead of on what Christ has said. For in Christ there is all of God in a human body; so you have everything when you have Christ, and you are filled with God through your union with Christ.

—Colossians 2:8-10

20 — YOU HAVE FORGOTTEN WHO YOU ARE

Jeannette claims from an early age she was engulfed by a sense of "nobodiness," the feeling she wasn't good enough. To feel a sense of purpose and accomplishment, her dad, who was a teacher, encouraged her to get a college degree and develop a career. She got accepted into an ivy league university and thought, "Now, my sense of nobodiness will go away." Not long after graduating, with honors, her feelings of competency disappeared. To improve her worth, she decided to go for her master's degree. Again, once attained, she felt like a nobody in a world with thousands of people who have master's degrees. She got a great job and decided to publish a book, believing finally a sense of well-being and worth would envelop her. The ecstatic feelings once again were short-lived.

One night she came across a Bible in the hotel room she was staying at. She flipped through it and then cried to God, "What must I do to feel saved and worthy?" The Bible revealed the truth to her:

"God saw all that he had made [Jeannette], *and it was very good"* (Genesis *1:31).* As she began studying God's Word, she learned the secret to feeling accepted and worthy is not filling her soul with things from the outside, but filling herself with God Himself.

† *When you look into your mirror each day, what statements about yourself are reflected back to you— "I feel like ..."*

THE INNER ABUSER

As we move from childhood onward, we soak up like crazy what we see, hear and are told—by our family, peers, teachers and mass media—molding our belief system which becomes second nature to us. The cultural context we soaked up so innocently in our preschool years is there in the background of our adult lives all the time, operating in our minds behind the scenes, like the "great and powerful wizard of Oz"—before he was exposed by Toto the dog.

Many of us are carrying around negative messages from those years about ourselves. If a parent or teacher told us we weren't very smart or just average, or worse, their words exerted a powerful influence. When we become adults, the messages are so ingrained we don't question them.

These toxic labels we give ourselves are swirling around in our minds. They are our *inner abuser:* the unconscious voice that calls us names today *incompetent, ugly, fat, stupid, unlovable, worthless.* The inner turmoil will continue to lower our self-worth and intrude unless we get rid of the inner abuser. It's not easy and it takes time. But God's power can prevail.

YOU AREN'T WHO YOU THINK YOU ARE

Soren Kierkegaard, back in the 1800's, claimed every human being thinks: *I wish to be someone other than who than I am; to have a different self.*

So, I try to make myself into someone different. He believed the pain and despair crushes us when we negate and shun our true selves, *but* the pain will evaporate when we stop denying who we really are and uncover our true nature. He stressed it is our responsibility to find our true essence and purpose in life. This is our mission. And God can't wait to show us who we really are!

In the classic Disney movie, *The Lion King,* Simba's dead father says to Simba, "You have forgotten who you are and so have forgotten me. Look inside yourself, Simba. You are more than what you have become. You must take your place in the Circle of Life."

To you God says, "You are more than you think you are." God always sees us as we can be, not as we are. Our real self hasn't died. It's just gone underground. There's nothing we can do to establish our worth. It's already been established by your Creator.

When Michelangelo was asked how he created a piece of sculpture, he said the statue already existed within the marble, giving God credit for creating his work. He believed his job was to get rid of the excess marble that surrounded God's creation. So, it is with us. Our job is to allow the Holy Spirit to remove all toxic thinking that surrounds our perfect selves. God created us to shine! We've been set apart to do great things. Scripture confirms us,

> *God created man **in his own image**, in the image of God he created him; male and female he created them. God blessed them …God saw all that he had made, and **it was very good** (Genesis 1:27-28; 31).*

A Randy Glasbergen comic goes, "Your resume here says that you are created in the image of God. Very impressive!" If someone has abused you, their misusing you to satisfy his/her own selfishness does not negate or change who you are—a valuable human being— worthy of love and respect. You wear a spiritual label, "Handmade by the Lord." Because we're made in the amazing image of God, *what we already are* is adequate to meet our needs and any crisis we may confront.

When Jesus begins to change our identity, we acknowledge that we're not who we thought we were supposed to be, or who we pictured ourselves being. We come to the place where we recognize that our value is not dependent on other people's opinions, our performance, titles, appearance, achievement or who we know.

The phrase "Christ in me" is used quite often in the Bible (John 14:20; 17:23; Galatians 2:20). Our worth comes from our *position* in Christ—not our *condition* in this world. We are not our weakness, our addictions, nor our fear, anger, shame or depression. There is Love and Beauty within us, and every day we need to be reminded of who we really are, thereby, changing our thinking patterns.

† *Claim God's Word, "I belong to Christ and have become a new person. The old life is gone; a new life has begun!" (2 Corinthians 5:17) Describe your emotional response to this good news.*

THE BEHAVIOR AND CUSTOMS OF THIS WORLD

Ralph Waldo Emerson wrote, "To be your true self in a world that is constantly trying to make you something else is the greatest accomplishment." This is our task—to implement Romans 12:2 through God's power:

> *Don't copy the behavior and customs of this world, but let God transform you into a new person by changing the way you think. Then you will learn to know God's will for you, which is good and pleasing and perfect.*

When my own dad stated to the entire family that I was "fat," and routinely scolded me about my appetite and weight (called fat-shaming), he was really saying, "Let me help you see what's wrong with you." His method didn't help. In addition to being fat-shamed, I created a picture of my ideal self from a worldview from models in magazines—possessing a body shape image that was impossible to attain. Conformed to the worldly kingdom, I ended up in a life-and death physical struggle driven by the "behavior and customs of this world." When I saw another skinny person or model, I "knew" for certain I wasn't thin enough. You could have told me my body shape was perfect, but it wouldn't have done any good because I was entangled in a false belief system I'd created. My brain suppressed the truth about healthy body image; instead I experienced unhealthy body image. *I held onto false information which didn't translate into transformation.*

The world demands we embrace and follow its values, which I did. The problem I had with my appearance had nothing to with my "body" but had everything to do with my "mind." James 1:24 states, *"You see yourself* [hear the truth] *and forget what you look like."* This is how we're conformed to the "behaviors and customs of this world."

All the untruths that have infiltrated our brains over our lifetimes are "the behavior and customs of this world." Every message, every mental image, and every internal voice that tells us we're something other than who God says we are; anything meant to steal, kill and destroy, is "the behavior and customs of this world." Every time I forget God's faithfulness and the special messages He's given me, I get sucked back into the behaviors and customs of this world. This is why we must learn to interrogate and capture deeply embedded lies and misbeliefs: *"We take captive every thought to make it obedient to Christ."*

A PARADIGM SHIFT

Let me ask you a question: Do you believe God was an inept workman when it came to creating you? If you said yes, you've been gravely deceived. Show me in the Bible where it says you're ugly, unlovable, incompetent, worthless, or fat? It doesn't say that. Joshua be Levi wrote, "A procession of angels pass before a human being where he or she goes, proclaiming, "Make way for the image of God." Reflect on each statement:

- You need not change yourself as much as you need to begin to understand how God has wired you.
- Who you are hasn't changed despite your history.

- You're not defined by the things you suffered or the labels which have been put on you.
- Bad choices or behavior doesn't equal bad person.

The truth about you is:

You were dead because of your sins and because your sinful nature was not yet cut away. Then God made you alive with Christ, for he forgave all our sins. He canceled the record of the charges against us and took it away by nailing it to the cross (Colossians 2:13-14).

Sometimes I don't think we really grasp the enormity of these verse; I don't. Everything you've done—past, present and even future—has been forgiven and nailed to the cross. As far as God is concerned, it never happened; its wiped clean off your record. Romans 3:22 tells us, "**We are made right** *with God by placing our faith in Jesus Christ. And this is true for everyone who believes, no matter who we are.*"

It's a fact: *Knowing and believing God's Word will change a person's life.* It will shift your self-identity. Before we can actually experience God's Word, we have to have faith. If we don't have faith in the author of the Word, then we won't experience much change. It's been said, "We tend to experience what *we expect* to experience." With a more biblical understanding of ourselves, we can experience a new self and be content with only seeking God's acceptance.

If this knowledge remains immaterial and we stick with our own perceptions, we won't be able to adequately deprogram our brains of misbeliefs; our true identity will never permeate our mind and become part of our lives. *For real mind renewal and transformation to occur, we need to experience who we are as defined by God.* We must *experience* what He says about us concretely and vividly.

✝ *Describe how it makes you feel to know that if you don't believe what God says about you in His Word, in essence you're calling Him a liar.*

21 — "JESUS PLUS NOTHING"

Five-hundred people were asked, "If you could see into the minds of others, what would you want to know?" What these people wanted to find out most is *what other people thought of them.*

In the Talmud (Old Jewish Law) it is written, "We do not see the world as it is, we see it as we are." Sadly, too many of us have a skewed sense of the world and ourselves, thereby believing *I am only as good as the number of "likes" I get on Facebook and Instagram.* If we want to heal from toxic thinking patterns, we have to understand that if God accepts us just as we are—which He does—then we don't need anybody else's acceptance.

"Acceptance" means we seek the approval and/or favor from another human being. For most of us, including myself, we desire to feel accepted by others. Validation fills the void. After all, God created us to belong to a community. Too many of us measure ourselves on the "favorable reception" ruler. In his book, *Dealing with the Rejection and Praise of Men,* Bob Sorge is direct and doesn't back down from his point of view,

> When we realize we are accepted and embraced by the great God of the universe, the acceptance of people becomes secondary. All I really need is His acceptance. When I have that, I can face rejection from anyone. This is how Jesus lived. He had the Father's acceptance so He didn't need anyone else's to give Him a sense of self-identity.
>
> When the Father said, *"This is my Son, whom I love; with him I am well pleased" (Matthew 3:17),* I can imagine Jesus's heart response being something like, "That's all I need! Just to know You approve of My life, Father, is enough for Me. Now I am complete and can rest in Your affection and approval. I don't care who rejects Me, as long as I know You accept Me!" Jesus knew He couldn't depend upon the acceptance of man, for men are fickle in their fallenness. The only acceptance that Jesus allowed to feed His spirit was the Father's.

As long as we look to flesh and blood for our approval, we will be snared by seasons of frustration and disappointment. My message is: *Jesus plus nothing.* When I have Him, I truly need nothing else. When I have His endorsement, I need no one else's. When I have His approval, I need no other source. His acceptance alone is enough.

I am not advocating an independent spirit. The Lord has called us to walk in inter-dependence with fellow Christians. We need other members. We look to each other for encouragement, counsel, prayer support, practical help, wisdom, perspective, for correction, etc. But we ought not look for others to be our sole source of acceptance. That comes from God alone.

It is a sign of maturity when we can receive correction without interpreting it as rejection. I am convinced this is one of the greatest challenges of Christian maturity: to make myself vulnerable to your kindness and affection, while not allowing myself to be penetrated by your rejection.[63]

✝ *Finish these sentences:*
- *I seek acceptance by …*
- *I seek acceptance when …*

COMPLETE IN HIM

Melanie confessed, "If I hadn't so desperately wanted Josh's approval of me as a wife, mom and lover, I might have seen the truth sooner."

Why do certain relationships hurt so much? Because we suffer rejection when we look for someone else's approval and acceptance but don't get it. If I desire your favor, I open myself up to your rejection.

Let's say your earthly dad has refused to recognize you most of your life. You still wear the battle wounds because no matter how hard you tried to get his favor, all you got was rejection upon rejection. As a "good Christian" you chose to forgive your dad. Then you see him at a family gathering. As is his nature, he is emotionally abusive, tearing you down. Now every wound from the past gets ripped up all over again. Once again, you're back in that place of feeling crushed, depressed and rejected by dad.

Maybe this scenario happens when your ex-husband picks up your kids for the weekend. There are hordes of situations where this happens. The critical question is: *To whom are you looking as the source of your acceptance?* It may be a number of people depending on your role. For example, when you are in the role of wife and mother, you may be looking for your husband's approval. When you are a student, you may be looking for your teacher's acceptance. Or, when you're at church, it may be your pastor's approval.

I encourage you today to decide to receive God's acceptance into your soul. It's all you really need. When our heavenly Father approves of us, then other people can call us names and tell us how bad we are—it won't wound because our spirit is being nurtured and fed by the Father's Spirit. This is a great challenge for each one of us, including me. We can get there if we remain connected to God. The key is deciding that He is going to be our sole source of acceptance.

Scripture tells us that we are "complete" in Him (Colossians 2:9-10). Dictionary.com defines "complete" means *to lack nothing; be full; finished; to make perfect*. When we are *complete* in God's acceptance then we should no longer crave any other earthly person's acceptance. Their rejection can no longer wound us.

Recognize: If man's acceptance will build you up, then man's rejection will tear you down. It appears then *the only way to close the door to another person's 'kick in the teeth' is by closing the door to needing and depending upon another person's acceptance and praise.*

Jesus said, *"No one can serve two masters. Either he will hate the one and love the other, or he will be devoted to the one and despise the other"* (Matthew 6:24). No one can get through life on other people's praises. O. Hobart Mower said, "It is the truth we ourselves speak rather than the treatment we receive that heals us." You must decide: God or man.

† *Consider today who is your master (or masters). Name the people you are looking to as the source of your acceptance.*

His Word: The Source of Our Acceptance

A fable goes: A mother tiger died giving birth to a cub. A pack of goats came upon the baby tiger and, sensing its plight, invited the cub to join the pack. As months went by the baby cub took on all the characteristics of a goat, even though he was a tiger by nature.

One day the king tiger came through the forest where the pack of goats lived. He stumbled across the tiger that was acting like a silly goat. He roared, "What is the meaning of this masquerade? Why are you behaving in such a different way?"

All the cub knew was to bleat and nibble at the grass. Then the king tiger figured out the problem: This little creature had no idea who he was. The king took him to the river and let him see for the first time a reflection of himself. "See. You are not really a goat. You are one of us," the king tiger said. Then he said, "Follow me, little one. I will help you become the grand thing you already have it in you to be!"

If we desire to experience our true new self, we have to create and install new experiences in our minds that confirm our God-given identities. Let your Creator show you your true nature; let Him show you are a worthy person deserving of love and approval regardless of what someone else has told you. Finding out how you've been designed and how God feels about you may be the most surprising discovery you'll ever make. It will provide immunity against criticism and rejection.

When we start to input the truth about ourselves, the brain will produce positive feelings versus negative ones—which means less thoughts we have to capture. *What is true of the brain's programming process is also true of its reprogramming process: it requires an event.* We need to align ourselves with God and His Word to create an event that deeply communicates truth. The more we meditate and visualize scriptural truths about ourselves, the more we'll believe them; the more we'll program ourselves for successful change. Negative thought patterns will begin to lose their power and in time will disappear. It's time to download these truths about ourselves into our brains and minds. Get ready for a paradigm shift.

- I am beautiful (Song of Songs).
- I am "complete" because God lives in me (Colossians 2:9-10).
- I have the highest possible value (Psalm 8:5; Genesis 1:27).
- I am fearfully ("awesome") and brilliantly made (Psalm 139:14).
- I am born of God. The evil one cannot touch me (1 John 5:18).
- I am the apple of God's eye (Deuteronomy 32:9-10).
- I am a beloved child (Ephesians 5:1)
- I am brand new (2 Corinthians 5:17).
- I am a pearl of great value (Matthew 13:45)
- I am a bounty of sparkling jewels (Isaiah 54:11-12).
- I am God's child and Christ's friend (John 1:12; 15:15).
- I am forgiven. My sins have been taken away (Ephesians 1:7).
- I am free from condemnation (Romans 8:1-2).
- I am a conqueror (*a survivor*; Romans 8:37).
- I cannot be separated from the love of God (Romans 8:38-39).
- I am a saint (1 Corinthians. 1:2).
- I am holy, blameless, covered with God's love (Ephesians 1:4).
- I have the favor of God (Proverbs 8:35)
- I am one spirit with Jesus (Galatians 3:28; 1 Corinthians 6:17).
- I am the salt and light of the earth (Matthew 5:13-14).
- I am blessed with every spiritual blessing (Ephesians 1:3).
- I have been adopted as God's child (Ephesians 1:5-6).
- I am God's work of art; His masterpiece (Ephesians 2:10).
- I have direct access to God (Ephesians 2:18; 3:12).
- I am confident because of God's work in me (Philippians 1:6).
- I can do anything through Christ's strength (Philippians 4:13).
- I am God ambassador and disciple (2 Cor. 5:20; Matt. 28:18-20).

To truly experience transformation, I suggest:

- As you read each statement, stop and observe how you think and feel about the truth. (Notice each statement begins with "I am" and not a negative like, "I am not …" *I am* speaks self-confidence; *I'm not*, doesn't.)
- Each day meditate and hold your thoughts for at least 12 minutes on one or two statements and look up the referenced Scriptures.
- Ask yourself: "What would a person with this belief naturally think and do?"
- Create in your mind a new experience by *visualizing it as reality*.

Don't worry if you can't fully grasp these truths about yourself, none of us can. Yet it is important that you *act on what God has said about you*. The next time a toxic memory pops up, pair that negative message or belief with the truth of Scripture, thereby, *creating a new event*. Simply reply, "Soul, you're wrong! God doesn't make junk. I'm incredible and amazing because I'm made in the image of God Almighty. I'm His self-portrait, beloved and free to be me!"

THE "NEW YOU"

When we hear the words "new you" we tend to think of something health and beauty oriented. Not surprising, God's got a different take on the "new you." Even though we're all born with the DNA from our family tree, when Christ comes into our lives God says, *"I will give you a new heart and put a new spirit in you … (Ezekiel 36:26)*. He unites us to Himself so that we're remade in His image (John 17:21). A new dynamic happens—we get God's spiritual DNA (so to speak) and we come to life: *"… you are in me, and I am in you" (John 14:20)*—but my baggage (past wounds and toxic self-talk) has to be opened, looked at, then dumped at His feet. Try these exercises:

1—Write a goodbye letter to the woman you are leaving behind. Then write another letter to your current self from your future self (choose the time frame: 6 months; 1 year; or 5-years in the future). *Where are you? What are you doing? Describe how well is the "new you" doing.* Never forget Jesus's promise, *"Everything is possible for him who believes"* (Mark 9:23).

2—If you are in a class setting, you should have received a handout at the beginning of class with a mirror and several "I am …" statements. You will now receive a blank mirror. Write on each line what you now see in your mirror—even if you're struggling to believe it.

Set Your Mind Free with Forgiveness

Then Peter came to him and asked, "Sir, how often should I forgive a brother who sins against me? Seven times?"
"No!" Jesus replied, "seventy times seven!"

–Matthew 18: 21-22

22 – The Dreaded "F" Word

When your brother has been gunned down by local militia, where can you find the strength to forgive? When your mother has been gang-raped, where can you find the ability to not retaliate? When you hold in your arms the lifeless body of your slaughtered child, where can you find the conviction to not pick up an AK-47? –Miroslav Volf[64]

A reporter wrote, "Never before has there been such a need to forgive what seems to be the unforgivable." Do you agree?

Sometimes the offenses committed against us were so horrid it's difficult not to desire revenge, even hate the person. How do we know when a particular act crosses the line and requires our forgiveness? Our reaction is the best clue.

- Are you walking around with a permanent clenched fist?
- Are you obsessing over the hurt?
- Are you plotting a revenge strategy? Is there hate in your heart?
- Do you subtly give the person the cold shoulder, or express an uncooperative spirit?

Do you want to get through to the other side of your pain? There is a way—it is found in forgiveness. Psychologist Gregory Jantz wrote,

> If the child of the past and the adult of the present are to integrate fully into the person of the future, there comes a time when both must release the hurts of the past. This doesn't mean you forget what's been done to you, but that you forgive those responsible, whether they deserve your forgiveness or not. Forgiveness is the final destination on your healing journey. The road that lies beyond is one of health.[65]

For many, the word *forgive* is the ultimate "F" word. Yet, God wants us to forgive because He has forgiven us (Colossians 3:3). He wants us to show mercy to others because He has shown mercy to us. In return, we are released from the bondage of unforgiveness. And it is a proven prescription for overall health and happiness! *Forgiveness can mean a radical change in mind*—a mind change that is so deep it changes us on many levels.

Although revenge seems to be a natural instinct, there is one big reason to resist it: it becomes obsessive. We find ourselves ruminating endlessly on the offense. The cost is devastating and destructive since we only wound ourselves. As the classic saying goes, "Don't let anyone rent space in your head for free."

Also understand that forgiving is *not* the same as "pardoning." Pardoning releases people from punishments or the consequences due them; forgiveness doesn't.

Forgiveness is not about the other person—it's about us—and all the benefits we can receive spiritually, emotionally and physically: *healthier relationships, greater spiritual and psychological well-being; less anxiety, stress, and hostility; lower blood pressure; fewer symptoms of depression and cardiovascular disease; a lower risk of: substance abuse, cancer, hormonal changes, immune suppression, arthritis, and possibly impaired neurological function and memory.* This is a powerful reason why God desires we forgive. And it is an expression of self-love and respect for our bodies.

Let me add that it is important to forgive what is yours to forgive. For example, if the offender wounded both you and your sister, you are responsible for forgiving the offender for what he/she did to you. Your sister is responsible for accepting her own injuries and working through her own forgiveness. You sort your injuries into your pile, the other person puts their injuries into their own pile. The same goes if your child is humiliated by a teacher, for example. It's natural to want to rescue. The humiliation belongs to your child, as painful as that is to endure. If we focus on someone else's pain, then we're not looking at our own pain. By involving ourselves in someone else's battles, we are delaying expressing our full feelings and also delaying the decision to forgive.

If you are an abuse survivor: When it comes to the subjects of forgiveness and confrontation, abuse survivors attach very different meanings and emotions to these subjects. No two women will handle them quite the same. Her internal and external sense of safety largely hinges upon her environment, circumstances and mental health. Personal restoration is always the first step to healing; forgiving an abuser is second; and confrontation, third. If you haven't done the necessary healing work, then forgiveness can feel premature, which can make you feel revictimized.

† *If you are struggling to forgive someone, describe how this introduction to forgiveness has resonated with you. What is going through your mind right now?*

23 — THE KEY TO FORGIVING

In *The Passion of the Christ*, a film that broke box-office records, the audience witnesses an according-to-the-Bible account of Jesus's last hours on this earth. The film centers around His arrest, trial, torture, crucifixion and resurrection, events commonly known as "the passion." If you saw this on film, no doubt, like me, you were shaken up when you realized what your Savior went through for you. Moviegoers felt His deep passion of love for them. I certainly did.

Jesus underwent a horrific torture and humiliation for our sins. What the movie didn't show was the horrific details of an actual crucifixion. Crucifixion was one of the most disgraceful forms of death and most dreaded methods of execution in the ancient world. The method of crucifixion was so brutal that I refrain from describing it in detail. Let me just say Jesus was beaten horrifically and His body torn from head to toe. And the soldiers far surpassed their orders in maliciously violating Jesus. To further shame the victims the Roman soldiers nailed them to the cross naked. Yet as Jesus hung nailed to the cross, He advocates something that stuns us, *"Father, forgive them. They don't know what they're doing"* (Luke 23:34).

Imagine having someone humiliate, ridicule, abandon, reject and torture you, and then drive stakes into your hands. Would you feel like praying for them? No way! Scripture says, *"He did not retaliate when he was insulted, nor threaten revenge when he suffered. He left his case in the hands of God, who always judges fairly"* (1 Peter 2:23).

Human nature calls for revenge and retaliation. Not Jesus. He didn't yell from the cross, "I hate you all!" even though He had every reason to be righteously angry. Sinless, He did nothing to deserve crucifixion. These three important words, "Father, forgive them," modeled what He taught people about forgiveness and loving their enemies.

JUDGING FAVORABLY

Jewish culture has emphasized the need to "judge favorably" for thousands of years. The rabbis declared that "judging others in favorable terms" is as important as visiting the sick, praying, or teaching the Scriptures to your children. It's terribly difficult to change our perceptions, but if we ask God to help us see the situation differently, we can change our perceptions—we can judge favorably. Deuteronomy 1:16-17 states,

Hear the disputes between your brothers and judge fairly ... Do not show partiality in judging; hear both small and great alike. Do not be afraid of any man, for judgment belongs to God.

Jenna conveyed to her therapist, "I now realize the person who hurt me is a victim and suffering with his own pain. He didn't realize he caused me suffering because he was too blinded and wounded himself." We can refuse to let the person's evil actions control our thoughts: "You no longer have access to my emotions. I'm free!"

The fact is: When someone is cruel he/she is usually afraid. Many psychotherapists agree that *shame-based fear*—the fear of never feeling noticed, of not feeling loved or belonging, nor having a sense of purpose, is a large reason for an offender's behaviors. What we choose to forgive is the flawed human being who did a very bad thing (or things) as a consequence of their own wounding and flawed belief system.

Scripture reminds us: *"For all have sinned and fall short of the glory of God. ... There is no one righteous, not even one"* (Romans 3:10;23). It's never a black and white issue. We forget we have a limited perspective. Rather than see the offender's behavior as something malicious directed at us, we should see them for what they are—a broken, sinful human being like all of us.

† *Describe how "judging favorably" feels to you at this moment.*

JUSTICE IS IN GOD'S HANDS

Many of us find it difficult to let go and forgive because we believe the person will get away with their offense, particularly if no penalty exists. For a couple years I took martial arts (Hapkito). One

technique I learned was to sidestep my attacker rather than resist him. The energy of the attack then turns back to the attacker. Forgiveness works the same way. Our power lies in remaining nonreactive. When we attack (verbally or nonverbally) we initiate a war that no one wins.

It helps to remember: No one ever gets away with sin. The Bible says God is the God of judgment; that God is a good Judge. He's a better judge than we are and knows every person better than we know them. The Bible provides numerous promises that God will take care of the offenders.[66] We're not responsible for them. So, we don't have to live with a bitter root of anger or hate, or plot schemes of retaliation. We can let go of the person and ask God to deal with them, which as "the Judge" He will do perfectly. As someone said, "God doesn't need us to police the world."

- *"Do not take revenge, my dear friends, but leave room for God's wrath, for it is written: "It is mine to avenge; I will repay," says the Lord"* (Romans 12:19; 2: 5-11; 2 Thessalonians 1:6-10).
- *"The LORD will not leave the guilty unpunished"* (Nahum 1:3).
- *"I, the LORD … give all people their due rewards, according to what their actions deserve"* (Jeremiah 17:10).
- *"The eyes of the LORD are everywhere, keeping watch on the wicked and the good"* (Proverbs 15:3).

Most often our desire is the offender be punished immediately. Why does God seem to wait so long? The Bible reveals that God doesn't change—sin still results in death; *but* in His grace and mercy God is giving offenders time to repent. Second Peter 3:9 reminds us, *"The Lord … is patient with you, not wanting anyone to perish, but everyone to come to repentance."*

What we know about God's character is that the purpose behind judgment is growth and not condemnation. God judges us in order to teach us something, not throw His mighty finger in our face. Jesus didn't bark from the cross, "Just wait. You'll get yours!" Jesus chose not to charge them with their sin.

One last comment: Judging favorably doesn't mean keeping silent, as in "I'll just let God deal with him." The person must be always held accountable.

† *What does God want you to take away from this material and apply to your life?*

REINTERPRET

Harper Lee wrote, "You never really understand a person until you consider things from his point of view . . . Until you climb inside of his skin and walk around in it." No healthy and happy person wakes up one day and decides to hurt or abuse or offend another person. *Broken people hurt people.* And *broken people raise broken people.* Remember that any behavior—in others and ourselves—is rooted in learned, conditioned responses that served some purpose originally. And some people are born with a personality disorder.

Be open to reframe your belief about the person. What works for me is to try to see them as "sick" versus "bad." We don't tend to be angry at people who are sick. Or, as one therapist asks her clients, "What would your response be if the offender was your own child?"

Every person, including abusers and con artists, have worth in God's eyes, and Jesus paid a huge price for their freedom. To protect ourselves, society locks up the bad guys. People are still accountable for their actions. There are consequences to bad behavior. But followers of Christ are commanded, *and empowered*, to pray, forgive, have compassion and judge favorably (Colossians 3:12-13). *Then we are free to enjoy personal healing and restoration!*

Many of my prayers to God have been, "Help me change my mind toward this person and help me to try to see [*name*] as you see [*name*]." Martin Luther King, Jr. once said, "I have decided to stick to love … Hate is too great a burden to bear."

DOING THE BEST THEY CAN

Sara had been extremely angry at her mom for years because she didn't stop her step-brother, Allan, from molesting her. Mom knew, yet never said a word. Sara's also angry at Allan for sexually violating her. In her book, *Rising Strong,* social researcher Dr. Brené Brown asks the reader to pretend for a minute. She wrote, "What if you had it on the highest authority that the person who hurt you is doing the very best that he or she can do?"[67]

Do you feel immediate resistance? It would be natural. *I don't believe it.* "If God told you, Sara, that your mom did the best she could, given her circumstances, would you be able to forgive her? And your step-brother too? ... What if I told you Sara, that your mother was a victim of abuse, and that your brother had been forced to watch pornography with his father as a young boy?"

Sara responded,

> If this is true, then my mom probably was doing the best she could. And Alan probably didn't know better. ... I'd rather be filled with grief for these two people than angry and resentful. I don't excuse them for not being responsible, but now I understand why they did this. I guess I need to grieve the fact I'll never have a "normal" family. I need to love my mom for who she is, not for who she should have been.

Sara gave herself permission to let go of the bitterness, judging and the waiting for something different to happen. *Turning anger into grief* was how she came to forgive her mom and Alan. She said, "I've concluded that we're all doing the best we can. I know I am. This is how Sara "honored" her mother (Exodus 20:12).

When we consider the domino effect of generational sin and deep-rooted false beliefs, we should ask, "Was the offender doing the best he/she could do?" In many cases, the answer is yes. In other cases, the answer is no. This makes me wonder, "Does a mentally unstable person do the best they can, or an addict, given their brain is not functioning correctly? What about an evil person?"

"Doing the best you can" is not the easiest course of action, but it is the most Christ-like. I now realize my dad's past hurtful remarks were his way of saying, "Let me help you see what's wrong with you so you can change and be a better person."

What we're being asked to do, through Christ's power, is begin to understand the situations and limitations the offender labored under, recognize some goodness in them, and feel a little compassion, not only for the hard journey they had, but also for any pain we may have caused them.

DIMINISHING THE POWER OF UNFORGIVENESS

Dr. Michael Lyles wrote, "Forgiveness detaches us from becoming the emotional hostages of others and is the key to restoration, even if those who hurt us knew what they were doing." The benefit of reframing the event is we are adding a positive image (memory) to the negative one, thereby diminishing its power to incapacitate us.

We can choose to see the person as guilty or ignorant. If we choose ignorance, in essence, we're saying: *I release you to God because I will no longer be emotionally manipulated by the memory of this or the emotions it activates.* At the same time, I need to accept the person's imperfections and let go of any expectations. High expectations only lead to disappointment. (Judging favorably doesn't only apply to the issue of forgiveness. It applies to any person who has a propensity to disappoint us—a parent, friend, spouse, leader, pastor, counselor or mentor.) Consider what God has told us,

- *"Shouldn't you have had mercy on your fellow servant just as I had on you?" (Matthew 18:33)* …
- *"Make allowances for each other's faults and forgive anyone who offends you. Remember, the Lord forgave you, so you must forgive others" (Colossians 3:13).*
- *"Don't you realize that you become the slave of whatever you choose to obey? You can be a slave to sin, which leads to death, or you can choose to obey God, which leads to righteous living" (Romans 6:16).*

Want to make the devil mad? Pray for your offender! *"Pray for those who persecute you" (Matthew 5:44).* For those of us in pain, one of the most appropriate expressions of extending mercy is to pray for the offender's healing. It requires asking God for a heart to do so.

✝ ✝ ✝

We live in an amazing world that is not designed to prevent suffering. We've got to trust in God's wisdom. We can choose to be a slave to bitterness, anger and unforgiveness—or to forgiveness and health. We can say "no more" to the power of pain, anger and hatred when we choose to judge favorably and work towards forgiving. When we see someone differently, their behavior doesn't change, but ours does. *We can be the change—when we're using our mind of Christ.*

JUDGING YOURSELF FAVORABLY

If you struggle with forging yourself—reframe, reinterpret and apply the same principles about judging another person favorably to yourself. No doubt, pain is the cause of your actions. Jesus says to you: *I love you. I will always forgive you.* If He sees you as forgiven and perfect then you need to see yourself with the same set of eyes. Forgiving yourself becomes possible when you believe what God says about you.

✝ *If you decide to NOT forgive someone else or yourself, answer these questions:*

- *Who stays emotionally imprisoned in this situation?*
- *Who continues to resent and shut down her own mind, heart and body?*
- *Whose life is limited by lack of forgiveness?*
- *What reasons do you have for NOT wanting to forgive?*
- *How do you feel justified?*

24 — A Renewed Perspective about Forgiveness

Damare, a small Sudanese boy, was taken as a slave after radical Muslims attacked his village. One day, Damare, who had been raised in a Christian home, snuck away to attend a church service. When he returned, his Muslim master was waiting for him. He accused Damare of committing a deadly act, "meeting with infidels." He dragged him into a field. He nailed his feet and knees into a large board while the boy cried out in agony. Miraculously rescued, Damare said he chose to forgive because "Jesus was nailed and forgave."[68]

What bold faith from a simple Sudanese boy! Like Damare, we're asked to complete the forgiveness process whether we feel like it or not. The truth is: Forgiveness is not a feeling. If it were, we would rarely forgive others because we would not "feel" like it. What we are talking about is choosing to take some kind of action that conflicts with our feelings.

There are two concepts of forgiveness we need to understand: *decisional* and *emotional*. Dr. Neil Anderson sums them both up in this statement, "Don't wait to forgive until you feel like forgiving. You'll never get there. Feelings take time to heal after the choice to forgive is made."[69]

DECISIONAL FORGIVENESS

The *decisional forgiveness* process usually comes first. It's not a feeling but *an act of my will* to obey God. I won't necessarily feel love for the person, especially if the offense was great. I choose to judge favorably; not to hold this injustice against the person or seek revenge. Instead, I choose to put my faith in God's justice.

Because God's nature is different than man's, God's people are expected, even required, to act differently than the rest of the world. Decisional forgiveness says, *I acknowledge the things you did, or did not do, that hurt me. I'm letting you off my hook and putting you on God's hook. I'm not going to let you and the unforgiveness hurt me anymore.*

EMOTIONAL FORGIVENESS

This is the process of replacing negative feelings with positive emotions. With decisional forgiveness, I choose to forgive you, but I'm unable to manage my negative emotions. I recognize that I cannot change my feelings without God's help. My heart needs time to catch up with my decision to forgive.

Decisional forgiveness takes place instantly and is based on Colossians 3:13: *"Forgive as the Lord forgave you."* On the other hand, emotional forgiveness can be a recovery process—a process of emotionally releasing and forgiving, time and again. As time goes on we often recognize new losses. We need to re-forgive because our losses tend to accumulate.

One last clarification—for someone who has deeply harmed you, there is no guarantee that you'll never return to older feelings. It is not uncommon to be triggered by something and then strongly feel the rage all over again. This is part of the natural fight/flight response. Rage is a healthy response to violation that is wired in us. For these complicated reasons it's vital to take your feelings immediately to Jesus and then talk to a safe person.

WHAT FORGIVENESS IS NOT

Many of us carry misconceptions and false beliefs about forgiveness which hinder us from mind renewal. Understanding what *forgiveness is not* is often the key to making the decision to forgive, and therefore, setting our minds free emotionally.

FORGIVENESS IS NOT LETTING THE PERSON OFF THE HOOK

Often an offender's actions destroy lives. Some choices produce serious consequences. This doesn't mean you don't hold the person accountable. King David committed adultery, then murdered a man to cover his sin. God judged David's sins and he paid dearly for his deceit for the rest of his lifetime. The consequences were irreversible. *Sin which has been forgiven and forgotten by God may still leave human scars, and often does.*

When God forgives us He's not saying past behavior is disregarded. U.S. laws demand people be held criminally responsible for their crimes. Forgiveness involves mercy and grace, but it also involves accountability. If we let them off the hook too easily, they may conclude the offense wasn't really that serious because the consequences were light. God sets penalties and He gives us the ability to do so.

Secondly, many people are very good at getting us to take the blame for their wrongs. Counselors have a saying, "When he looks at himself in the morning and sees his dirty face, he sets about washing the mirror." They must recognize it is their face in the mirror—admit their wrong, then ask for forgiveness.

FORGIVENESS DOES NOT EXCUSE, MINIMIZE OR JUSTIFY

Janna's parents demanded she forgive her brother for making her watch pornographic movies with him. She agreed and said, "He didn't know what he was doing," even though she believed he knew right from wrong.

Did you know the mind cannot accept a rationalization? When we carefully rationalize some behavior, we may convince ourselves at an intellectual level, but not at the emotional and spiritual level.[70] One of the greatest American writers, F. Scott Fitzgerald wrote, "There are open wounds, shrunk sometimes to the size of a pin prick, but wounds still."

You may be asked to forgive because your family wants you to. Families have a way of justifying or minimizing what's taken place. Many offenders want you to take responsibility for their behavior. Forgiveness is not saying, "It's no big deal." If it's no big deal, there's nothing to forgive.

FORGIVENESS DOES NOT FORGET

There is a word which cannot be associated with forgiveness: "forget" (as in "forgive and forget"). The fact is, we don't forget. Brain studies reveal whatever is significant to us is stashed away in our long-term memory.

Paul said, *"I forget what's behind …" (Philippians 3:13).* The biblical word "forget" in this context doesn't mean "put out of one's mind." It has the *meaning of letting go—not allowing the past experiences to dominate the future.* Many have used this verse to prod a person into silence about painful, unresolved issues of the past.

Furthermore, if someone is taught to be a "good Christian" and to forgive and forget, the offender, and others involved, may get the message the behavior is acceptable. We must understand God's reconciliation process: when we forgive, the offense is forgotten *as far as the relationship is concerned* because it's no longer relevant to the relationship. The memory isn't erased; the facts of the event aren't expunged. *We are choosing not to dwell on it anymore.*

FORGIVENESS IS NOT CONTACT OR A FUTURE RELATIONSHIP

Speaking of her husband, Annie said, "He told me he was sorry. I know I'm supposed to forgive and trust, but I can't let myself be hurt again. If I let him back in I know he'll hurt me again." Who said anything about letting him back in and trusting him? People are reluctant to forgive because they don't understand the difference between forgiveness and trust and reconciliation.

Forgiveness has to do with the past. The hurt person makes the choice to let the offense go. Trust and reconciliation have to do with the present and the future. *Forgiveness is not an expectation of a future relationship with the person.* No mere words can bring about a significant repair. *The offender must prove he/she's changed over time and are trustworthy.* They need time to take the steps required for true restoration. Sometimes it cannot be restored.

Annie finally realized she would relieve herself of the bitterness, resentment and pain, if she chose to forgive her husband for adultery, even though she had biblical grounds for divorce. She also learned that by making the decision to forgive her husband, this didn't change him; it didn't make him any more trustworthy. Until he could prove he was, she chose to separate from him and move on. She told him, "You hurt and wronged me, but I choose not to hold it against you. I trust God to judge you fairly … but I have to put a safeguard and boundary into place so this event doesn't happen again."

The definition of "trust" is: *What is important to me is safe with you in this situation (or any situation).* Conversely, "distrust" is: *What is important to me is NOT safe with you in this situation (or any situation).* Trust is always earned. To trust someone is to feel confident the person is who he/she appears to be. They must prove to be faithful, honest and have integrity. Therefore, it takes time to rebuild and requires patience. Research has shown that it can take up to 2-years to develop an authentic attachment bond when there *hasn't* been any type of hurt or betrayal. Therefore, the person who is working to change and earn your trust must be very patient with you; give you "all the time in the world" as they say.

Warning: If you believe this person has a personality disorder, or is a psychopath or dangerous, do not meet with him/her. In my opinion, you'll most likely be dragged right back into the same old mind games. You can forgive them, but for your safety you don't have to tell them you forgive them. You are in this good place now because of your distance away from this person.

FORGIVENESS IS NOT WAITING FOR AN APOLOGY

Some say, "I'll forgive him as soon as he says he's sorry." There are people who will never apologize. They will continue in their destructive, rebellious and foolish behavior. Others will be stubborn and never confess or admit their sin. Some will move away and others will die before they ever repent. We choose to forgive them anyway because we know it's God's desire.

The healing process for us and the repentance process for the offender, requires humility and talking about the offense. Healing evolves when we talk about the pain and have our feelings validated. The offender may ask, "Why do you keep bringing up the past? … How many times do I have to tell you I'm sorry! Let's just move on." These are indicators of lack of repentance. They're often saying they don't want to look at your wound or be accountable for what they did. When the person allows you to express your feelings and feels true sorrow—called "repentance," it's possible to move forward and *"forget what's behind."*

✝ *How has this "Forgiveness is Not" list made you more receptive towards forgiveness?*

25 – AUTHENTIC REPENTANCE = RELATIONSHIP REPAIR

A relationship can begin the process of restoration when the offender shows signs of humility and authentic repentance. I love Bruce Wilkinson's description: *"Repentance means you change your mind so deeply that it changes you."* This is not the same as remorse. When repentance is real, there is a groaning from the spirit that truly means, "I'm sorry. I don't ever want to do this again." The person is willing to look at the truth. Then a flow of completed forgiveness from the heart may begin to restore the relationship. Jesus told this parable called the Pharisee and the Tax Collector (See Luke 18:10-14). Scripture says,

One day Jesus told his disciples a story to illustrate their need for constant prayer and to show them that they must keep praying until the answer comes (v. 1) … Then he told this story to some who boasted of their virtue and scorned everyone else." (v. 9).

Two men went to the Temple to pray. One was a proud, self-righteous Pharisee, and the other a cheating tax collector. The proud Pharisee 'prayed' this prayer: 'Thank God, I am not a sinner like everyone else, especially like that tax collector over there! For I never cheat, I don't commit adultery, I go without food twice a week, and I give to God a tenth of everything I earn.' But the corrupt tax collector stood at a distance and dared not even lift his eyes to heaven as he prayed, but beat upon his chest in sorrow, exclaiming, "God, be merciful to me, a sinner." I tell you, this sinner, not the Pharisee, returned home forgiven! For the proud shall be humbled, but the humble shall be honored. (Luke 18:10-14)

Pharisees were regarded as the most devout religious group of men in Jesus's time. The name "Pharisee" comes from a root word that means "pure." These guys sought purity in *all* things. They were famous for their religious enthusiasm and piety (means a dutiful spirit of reverence for God). They believed they were morally superior to most other human beings. They had pride in themselves and disdain for others. Tax collectors were at the opposite pole. Considered dishonest and greedy, they were despised. Certainly, a repentant tax collector defied all the stereotypes of the day.

The surprise of the parable doesn't lie in the Pharisee's prideful attitude, but in the tax collector's response. He cries for mercy and grace, recognizing his brokenness. We're not told by Jesus what brought this man to his knees, but something brought him to that "hit rock bottom" or "come to Jesus" moment.

Toby was a faithful husband and good father, but had an erratic binge drinking problem. He would go on these binges and spend the family money and become verbally and physically abusive to his wife and kids. After beating his wife one evening (she had confronted him about spending their son's money for a sports uniform) their 12-year-old called 911 because her face was covered with blood. Toby was arrested for battery.

This event finally brought him to his knees and senses. Toby saw his wife's bruised face and he cried like a baby, vowing to never be violent again. He admitted he needed God in his life to change him. The next week a friend took him to a Celebrate Recovery meeting. With God's help, his life—and his family's life—moved in a new direction. It is possible the tax collector had a similar experience—an event made him aware of how low he had gotten.

Authentic repentance cannot be fabricated. It takes a lot of hard work. Luke 3:8 states, *"Prove by the way you live that you have repented of your sins and turned to God."* When someone is truly repentant, he or she will show evidence of a changed heart. Then there's a strong chance of reconciliation and restoring intimacy. Sometimes a person will try to bargain, "If you forgive me, then I'll get help." It doesn't work this way. Authentic repentance must come first—then reconciliation is possible.

With repentance comes restoration. Jesus tells us what going on behind the supernatural curtain when we repent: *"I tell you that in the same way there will be more rejoicing in heaven over one sinner who repents than over ninety-nine righteous persons who do not need to repent" (Luke 15: 7).*

✝✝✝

Here's my motivation for forgiving: Actress Sara Miles once said, "An unforgiving nature reflects in your face. Holding negative energy drags down the facial muscles, puckers one's frown and causes lines around the mouth. Working daily on forgiveness is the cheapest, most effective facelift in the whole wide world."

We need some humor when we're working through tough subjects. ☺

Put on the Mind of Christ

But we have the mind of Christ.
—1 Corinthians 2:16

26 — INVESTIGATE AND CAPTURE YOUR THOUGHT LIFE

Do you now believe: *Your thought life doesn't have to control you; you can control your thought life*? I hope so. It's been the objective of this study. We have power over what we believe and what we believe holds power over us—the power to thrive or be defeated. Even though we can't control our circumstances—life and people—we can control our reaction—thoughts and attitude—to those circumstances. It's never too late for a rewrite!

Our task is not only seeking the truth but living it out. What good are God's principles if they really don't change our lives? With this in mind, we're going to take everything we've learned about our toxic thinking patterns and apply five powerful steps to conquer them.

Scientists claim we don't just add facts to our memories, we *literally redesign our memories* with each new piece of information that we add and understand. You can choose to be a "deep thinker" and change your brain! [71] This means you think, feel and make choices in a repeated, intentional, deliberate way to induce positive emotional, behavioral, spiritual and relational change.

The following reflective investigative exercises will enable you to take your toxic thoughts captive and not allow anyone to capture you with *empty deceptive philosophies* and *corrupted deceitful desires*. God wants us to believe based on evidence, so get ready to learn to inquire and investigate your thoughts, and then set yourself free! (John 8:36) Commit to one, maybe two, steps per day.

Jesus must be at the center of this. So, make each step a conversation with Him. He'll help you see on paper what's whirling around in your mind—your reality. Remember, *it's the thought that's painful—not your life; not you!* … And doing these steps actually alters the brain's neuron and nerve cells, changing the way your brain works.[72] That's exciting! Philippians 2:5 tells us to *"Have this mind in you, which was also in Christ Jesus" (ASV).*

Step 1—State your belief about yourself.

We first want to *identify our predominant negative thought or belief.* We all have "internal perpetrators" in our minds—judgements about ourselves, about others, or situations which cause stress in our lives. For example,

- "I'm a failure; not good enough; hopeless."
- "Good things don't happen to people like me."
- "I can't do that; not compared to her."
- "My boyfriend is going to leave me."
- "Dad doesn't deserve my forgiveness."
- "My mother doesn't love me."

Write your thought or belief out just the way your mind is saying it. *This is your reality.*

Step 2— When I believe this thought, how do I feel and react?

Ask: *What's the impact on my life when I believe this thought?* Speak to the impact the belief has on your life. Use these questions as a guide:

- What *emotions* arise when you believe that thought? Talk about the suffering, frustration, anxiety, rage, sadness, discomfort; whatever you are feeling.

- What *physical* sensations arise as you think that thought (emotions affect us physiologically). For example, your blood pressure rises, experience insomnia, hands start to shake.

- How do you *act out* (the impact)? Do any obsessions or addictions surface when you believe this thought? Do you overuse alcohol, drugs, shopping, food, sex, television, or social media, for example?

- How do you *treat and talk to yourself* when you believe this thought? (Harsh self-talk is re-abusing ourselves. If someone used harshness as a method of control, we internalize that voice, which is now part of our self-talk.)

- Ask yourself, *"Who's voice is this?"* For example, is it me when I was 10-years-old? Is it my mother's voice?

- How do you *treat and talk to others* when you believe this thought?

This is your reality!

Step 3—How might I, and my life, be different without this thought? (Will this matter a year from now?)

By adding the power of our imagination, called "visualization" to a negative thought, we can move forward by rewriting an old mind script. Most often this thought has become our identity and can be difficult to visualize who we'd be without it.

In this step, take the time *to visualize your future without this thought—visualize yourself living out the truth. Who are you?* Also, *consider physiologically how you might feel.* For example, "I would have less colds." (Scientists have found that people with the highest levels of negative emotions are three times more likely to develop a cold than those having high levels of positive emotions.) Take the truth and create a vivid picture or movie of what this truth looks like for you personally. For example, if you are struggling with a fear, *visualize specific ways to overcome that fear/situation.*

Now the detective work begins. We want to answer, to the best of our abilities, this question: *Can I be absolutely certain it's true?*

In other words—*Is there (biblical) truth to support this belief? How can I find out? What more do I need to find out about myself, or the person(s)?* We take the time to inquire, look for proof and dig deeper. This is called "disputing." Put differently, "Am I looking at this all wrong?" "What are the facts?" (Deal with reality instead of perceptions.)

If your belief is based on another person's remark, ask yourself: *"Based on this person's character and flaws, can he/she really be believed?"* Getting second-hand information about a situation or person is not reliable. Getting clarity on why another person said or did what they did, requires getting their perspective firsthand and then *verifying that you've understood it correctly.*

What if the negative belief is true? Stated belief: "My father has never loved me." In your investigation, you find out that your father intentionally distanced himself from you because you reminded him of his "awful and noxious" ex-wife, your mother. Unfortunately, this is true. Instead of believing all the reasons why your father shouldn't love you, seek reality. *Do not take this out on yourself. It is his loss.*

- Give yourself credit for having the courage to seek the truth. No matter the outcome, you were brave, open and on the right path.
- You now have an explanation as to why you think a certain way and do the things you do. You can continue to move forward.
- Ask yourself: "Ok. My dad never loved me. What's the worst that can happen?"
- Reflect on Dr. Lisa Najavits's comment, "The most painful truth is better in the long run than the most positive lie."[73]

> **Step 5—Create a new belief; a new truthful thinking track.**

Once we recognize the toxic belief is false and an illusion, then we have to replace it with something. We create a new thought; a new and different thinking track; we replace destructive self-talk with truthful and compassionate self-talk. This is *not* an exercise in "positive thinking." It's learning "realistic thinking" and does wonders to heal our brains. The Bible gives us precise instructions:

> *Whatever is true, whatever is noble, honorable, whatever is right, whatever is pure, whatever is lovely, whatever is admirable—if anything is excellent or praiseworthy—think about such things. Whatever you have learned or received or heard from me or seen in me—put it into practice. And the God of peace will be with you (Philippians 4:8-9).*

The phrase "think about such things" is critical. In other words, "focus and keep your thoughts on" and "let your mind dwell on" these things which will enable us to lay down a new set of thought patterns. Notice the first quality mentioned to think on is truth. When we think on God's things, we are putting on the mind of Christ.

Oswald Chambers wrote, "If a saint lets his or her mind alone, it will soon become a garbage patch for Satan's scarecrows." That's a word picture! Satan *will* deceive the mind that chooses not to think on truth and the qualities in Philippians 4:8. Notice the outcome: *peace.* As we study truth and dwell on the good things, we will get better at spotting deception; we can find peace from our past.

I suggest these different methods depending on what the belief or situation is. *Each exercise is designed to move your mindset from hopeless to hopeful.*

1—Turn a Harsh Thought into a Compassionate Thought

Example 1—Using the previous example, "My father never loved me," turns into "My father didn't love me—not because of who I am or what I did—but because he hated my mother so much. His lack of love has nothing to do with me. He needs to see a therapist and work out his issues with Mom. I have a heavenly Father who loves me so much. He wants to be part of my everyday life. He will never ever leave me."

Example 2—You believe, "I'm such a loser!" *If your best friend made the same statement, how would you answer her or him?* Simply put, would you say you speak to yourself in the same way you do someone you respect and/or love, like your best friend or your child? Would you agree and tell her, "You're right! You're a huge failure"? No. You'd probably answer compassionately. Be your own best friend or child!

2—Redirect and Turn the Thought Around

Use the past tense when talking about your problem and future tense when talking about how your life will be positively different. For example,

- Change *if* into *when:* "If I get out of this depression" becomes "When I get out of this depression."
- Change *can't* into *not yet:* "I can't stop drinking" becomes "I haven't stopped drinking yet."
- "I can't cope," becomes "I can do this through God's power."
- Begin your sentences with: *I know how … I can … I have learned … I am able …*

Consider this: We dislike, even hate, in others what we often dislike or hate in ourselves. Turned around thoughts can be powerful when we discover that what we see on the outside; or see in another person, is really a projection of our own minds.

It is easy to see the wrongs in others that we are equally guilty of (Matthew 7:5; Romans 2:1). Life coach Iyanla Vanzant said that whenever there's a strong judgment about someone else, it's usually a cover up story we don't want to tell about ourselves. Think of a couple of people you dislike or who irritate you. It's likely you have the same feelings buried deep in your unconscious about yourself.

If your judgment about another person feels uneasy, ask yourself if you've hit on a belief *about yourself* that you haven't investigated yet. For example, "He should love me," turns around to "I should love myself." Or, "I can't live with this person any longer," turns around to "I can't live with myself any longer … and I need to gain some personal insight."

3—Change a Belief about a Situation

We ask, *"Is the situation changeable?"* Not all are: 69 % of conflicts involve unresolvable problems.[74] For example, Betsy's been trying to "fix" a bad habit of her sister's. She had to admit, "Darlene is never going to change without God's supernatural intervention. I can't fix her." Some situations are changeable. Then we list all the ways we can change the situation.

Make two lists: *Unchangeables* and *Changeables*. The *Unchangeables* are situations that cannot be changed; things we have no control over. For example, your dad molested your daughter. This is a fact and a prayer request. "God grant me the serenity to accept the things I cannot change." Express how each situation makes you feel.

Unchangeable (Prayer Request)	Makes Me Feel (Hopeless)	Changeable	Makes Me Feel (Hopeless)
Dad's controlling ways.	*I feel like I don't have a voice or a choice.*	I can set boundaries, speak up, move forward following God's lead and not dad's lead.	*I feel empowered.*
Ex-husband believes I'll always be an addict and a loser.	*I feel like a loser.*	I can get clean; choose my destiny: go back to school, get training, find new friends, etc.	*I feel confident; worthy.*

We can work on fixing, reframing or changing the *changeable;* what we have some control over. Let us let go of the *unchangeables* and turn them over to God to handle.

27 — PERSONAL APPLICATION "I'M A FAILURE."

What you believe is what you become ultimately. Too many women believe they are failures and have similar beliefs of unworthiness. I want women to uncover the evidence they are not a failure through this example.

1—Write down your judgement statement about yourself—your thinking error. For example, *"I am a failure at everything I do."*

2—When I believe this thought, how do I react (the impact)? What do I do when I feel this feeling? How do I behave? *"Feeling like a failure makes me feel like if I do anything it will be wrong. I feel depressed, like I'm the only one who struggles with this. This is my core belief."*

3—How might I, and my life, be different without this thought? *"Without this thought I'd be a more peaceful and confident person. I'd feel free, like a huge weight has been lifted off my back. I'd be healthier too."* Picture who you'd be without this negative thought. *I see myself a successful missionary for God and a conqueror.*

4—Question and investigate the truth of the thought. *Can I be absolutely certain that it's true—that I'm a failure?* Naturally your statement appears true because it is based on a lifetime of uninvestigated unconscious beliefs. Your parents may have said so, therefore, you say so. But *can you be absolutely certain it's true that you're a failure? Or did* *you draw a wrong conclusion about yourself based on your parent's opinion, and not truthful reality?*

Look for the proof and inquire deeper. *Is there truth to support this belief? Did God's Word say I'm a failure?* Answer: No! Scripture proves that if I have God's nature in me, then I'm not a failure; not inferior, but a person of great value! God said that:

- I'm fearfully ("awesome") and brilliantly made (Psalm 139:14).
- I've been created for a specific purpose (Psalm 139:13-16); there's a special, divine blueprint for my life (Jeremiah 29:11). (They'll not be small dreams!)
- I'm a conqueror (Romans 8:37).
- God will complete through me what He's called me to do (Philippians 1:6).
- I have a spirit of power, love and sound mind (2 Timothy 1:7).
- I can be conformed to the image of Christ—created to be a difference-maker in this world (Romans 8:29).
- "With Christ as my partner, there is no such thing as failure, only results" (Toni Sorenson).

To prove you're not a failure, focus your attention to some past successes you've had; and work with God to discover your unique blueprint. Write it all down. Look at everything you wrote. Then ask yourself if it's true that you're a failure; that you'll never amount to anything. The answer is NO! The evidence is clear and reveals your real worth.

5—Create a new belief; a new thinking track. Ask: *Can this thought be turned around? Can this situation be changed?* Yes. "I have special gifts and talents! I'm not a failure. There's something I can do that no one else can do! I've been chosen and appointed to bear good things (John 15:16)."

Every reaction or behavior comes from a single thought. When we begin to think with our minds of Christ, we in turn shape our world and truly begin to reflect Jesus's magnificent light! Don't get discouraged. Ask God for wisdom. The Bible assures us that He gives us a way to handle every situation:

> *By his divine power, God has given us everything we need for living a godly life"* (2 Peter 1:3); *When you are tempted, he will show you a way out so that you can endure (1 Corinthians 10:13).*

I can tell you personally that when we know God's plan for our lives He far exceed our wildest dreams! I would never have imagined that I'd have written this study, and would be a pastoral counselor and teaching you today. He has big dreams and plans for you too!

28 — BREAKING BAD HABITS AND ADDICTIONS

Habits and addictions run our lives.

When you've wanted to change a thought or behavior in the past, how often has "Don't do it!" worked for you? This reminds me of the Bob Newhart skit titled, "Just stop it!" (Newhart played a psychologist in the 1970s series *The Bob Newhart Show*.) His solution to every problem: "Just stop it!" Don't like your weight? Stop eating so much! Don't like hangovers? Stop drinking! As Dr. Phil says, "How has that worked for you?" Not so good?

Over the past 25-years, the success of the anti-smoking campaign has been achieved mainly by people changing the environments in which they live. Smoking has been reduced due to smoking bans, higher taxes, eliminating ads from TV, magazines, billboards and stores. These environmental changes made it more difficult to smoke and thus helped to break many people's habitual behavior patterns.

University of Southern California's research program has shown that habitual behaviors are grounded in a person's regular daily environment—they are cued and maintained automatically and unconsciously. They figured out that the best way to change behavior is to change the person's environment. In the case of good habits, we must learn to tie them to a regular place and time (recall *Step One: Create a Habit of Worship*). For the bad habits we want to get rid of, we must remove from our surroundings the cues and opportunities (the temptations) that support them.[75]

C. S. Lewis wrote, "In each of us there is something growing, which will be hell unless it is nipped in the bud." First Corinthians 10:23 states, *"You say, "I am allowed to do anything"—but not everything is good for you ... not everything is beneficial."*

One of the leading experts on the mind, Dr. John Bargh, advocates creating *mindful intentional goals*. For example, if I'm tempted to eat a big dessert or buy more clothes, then I basically tell myself that *I need* to eat healthy so I can feel stronger (my reward) or *I need* to save my money for my kid's future. It sounds pretty simplistic, but having a goal that you verbalize or visualize is a whole lot more powerful than "Don't eat the dessert or buy any more clothes."

We all have good intentions and really want to carry them out (which is why you're reading this book). Too many times our good intentions fall away because we really don't want to change or we fear change—we really want to keep eating desserts or buy more clothes. God will provide the power, we need to provide the intention. We've got to have the "want to." He promises us, *"I will instruct you and teach you in the way you should go; I will counsel you and watch over you" (Psalm 32:8).*

† *Reflect on what running guru Dr. George Sheehan said, "The body wants to do what it did yesterday. If you ran yesterday, it wants to run today. If you didn't, then it doesn't want to."*

From Habit to Addiction

When my feet hit the floor each morning, I promised myself that I wouldn't binge and purge on any food that entire day. Yet when the clock rolled around my body and brain were expecting—*demanding*—comfort food. Then my attitude and behavior changed dramatically. At this point all the rationalizations came flooding out: "One more day won't make that big a difference. I'll quit tomorrow." But this promise is never kept—tomorrow never came. This is one of those great intentions that was too powerful to overcome.

Dr. Larry Crabb wrote, "Whatever feels good, what seems to give us an immediate experience of life, we decide *is* life; we decide it is food for our souls, and we chase after it with all the excitement of a street person in the back alley rummaging through the fine restaurant's garbage."

Addictions—we've all got them. Me too! 1 Corinthians 10:13 states, *"The temptations in your life are no different from what others experience."* According to neuroscientist and psychologist Marc Lewis, "addiction" is a *habit* that grows and self-perpetuates relatively quickly when we repeatedly pursue the same highly attractive desire or goal. Addiction is unquestionably destructive, yet it is also uncannily normal; an inevitable feature of the basic human [flawed] design.[76]

In the world of addiction, there are two major categories: *addiction to substances,* which involves abuse of and dependency upon chemicals (the updated DSM now calls this "substance-use disorders") and *addiction to patterns of behavior,* called "behavioral or process addictions."

Multitudes of people are hooked on things that don't fit the addiction stereotype, such as wealth, health, TV, social networking, work, shopping, eating, smoking, reading/education, risk taking, jogging and religiosity. We can become addicted to people and being in love, as well as sports, people-pleasing, body worship (exercise, dieting, plastic surgery) collecting—even pain, anger, revenge, worry, chaos, and stress. Add to the list: technology, politics, celebrity worship, gaming, tattooing, tanning, love for pets.

Science proves that behavioral addictions can be just as severe as substance addictions. The thing is: Your brain doesn't care if you get pleasure from sex, drugs, social media, shopping, food, a person, or sugar. The brain has an insatiable appetite. Its reward system has one thing in mind—pleasuring our senses by causing massive amounts a feel-good neurotransmitter to start spilling into the brain's reward center. The result is decreased anxiety and a calming of the physical effects of the body's threat-response system.[77]

† *Do you see your "favorite thing" on this list of behavioral addictions?*

How Addiction Hijacks the Brain

No addiction ever comes out of the blue. Addiction of any kind simply means we are controlled; that our life is dominated by an obsession and craving for some influence or substance, regardless of negative consequences.

In our brain there are different types of chemicals or neurotransmitters which significantly shape all of our emotions, behaviors and moods. The right amount helps us think clearly, feel well-balanced, and cope with both emotional and physical stress and pain. Improper balances of transmitters contribute to diseases such as obsessive-compulsive disorders, anxiety, and many forms of depression.

Dopamine is a chemical that fires up in the brain triggering feelings of pleasure, passion, adventure, motivation, and reward. When we do something exciting or rewarding, it produces a feeling of exhilaration or pleasure—the "I've got to have it" feeling.

When God created the dopamine response it was for survival. Activities like eating, drinking, engaging in sex, and working, contribute to the survival of the human race. Therefore, our brains are programmed to encourage these behaviors by making them highly pleasurable (Eccl. 2:24-25).

It also helps to remember that the destructiveness of addiction does not lie in the things we're attached to. They are simply part of creation and God made them essentially good. The destruction lies in our bondage to them. (In Latin *addiction* means to "be enslaved by" or "bound to.")

The second part of 1 Corinthians 10:13 gives us all hope, *"And God is faithful. He will not allow the temptation to be more than you can stand. When you are tempted, he will show you a way out so that you can endure."*

YOU ARE A SLAVE TO WHAT CONTROLS YOU

In my past, I'd get the "high" I desired from the first two drinks. At that point I should have quit. But I never did. I couldn't. I'd continue to drink until I was belligerent, acting like a fool or sick. It was too hard to stop; self-control never worked. Then other things in life lost their appeal.

The problem is there is an action command going on in the brain that is difficult to turn off. This is why will-power and "Tomorrow, I'll stop" doesn't ever work. When self-control is unraveling, the *dopamine synapses* are buzzing throughout the brain (*striatum*) and immediate rewards fill the mind.

We know emotional distress and chaos initiates the search for addictive rewards, intended to provide relief and comfort … for a while. Addiction escalates because we're not able to self-soothe and regulate uncomfortable emotions, and no consequences have surfaced (yet). So, we learn to push the anxiety away through an addictive behavior, usually something that provides some kind of soothing or narcotization (numbing out). Like myself, many discover their toxic feelings can be most effectively stopped through substance abuse, an eating disorder or some other obsessive behavior.

WHAT FIRES TOGETHER—WIRES TOGETHER

There's a saying, *what fires together (in the brain) wires together.* Anything that has *emotional significance* to us will wire together. For example, the first time I binged, my brain produced a firing pattern. For each binge that followed, this new firing pattern got reinforced and connected to regions all over my brain. Prior to each subsequent binge, when I'd visualize how good the food would taste, the synaptic networks would flash over my brain—"urgent." Now my entire brain had been affected and was changing rapidly. Thoughts, feelings and action patterns got altered.

While these busy synapses were strengthening some networks and forming a "binge configuration," other previously used networks were shutting down with misuse, such as the good habit and motivation of going to class each day and connecting with my best friend. Other goals like graduating, calling Mom more, and going to church, began to fade and eventually became unimportant. In other words, there's a breakdown in communication between the part of the brain that pursues goals and the part that can control that pursuit.[78] This is why it's important to 'nip a bad habit in the bud' by creating a mindful intentional goal—before it becomes an addiction.

The craving intensifies when the *midbrain* sends the *dopamine* up to the *accumbens*. *I really want it—and right now! I know it will make me feel good or calm … and nothing else matters.* This is called "desire." It soothes us; pleases us—and becomes a vicious destructive cycle. What once created pleasure soon causes anxiety. And its only relief—more of our favorite thing. It's like being possessed by the desire. Peter 2:19 states, *"For you are a slave to whatever controls you."* It all becomes part of the same familiar pattern.

THE POWER OF REPETITION

Repetition is the engine that strengthens and perpetuates what has captured our desire. Repeated experiences become first a habit, then an addiction, becoming robust networks in the brain, becoming more efficient with repetition. So, the habit gets deeper. The more the action is repeated the stronger it gets. It wires itself with others habits which get stronger and stronger causing more brain changes. Wants or desires become needs. Proverbs 21:17 says, *"You're addicted to thrills? What an empty life! The pursuit of pleasure is never satisfied"* (Msg).

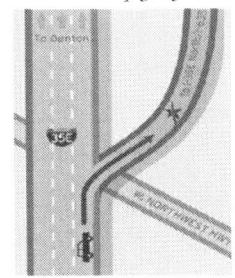 Think of a dozen little roads being replaced by a giant freeway … but every freeway has a number of off ramps. We need to discern the right and truthful off-ramps. Some lead to God while, others lead to the "god of this world."

In *Step One: Create a Habit of Worship*, we learned that the secret to creating a healthy habit is to create a cue and reward system that fuels the desire to repeat the process. We must choose to do the hard work of identifying cues and triggers and rewards that pull us unconsciously into a bad habit or an addiction. We need to be clear on the rewards they "appear" to offer, and then change how we do things. For the bad habits we want to get rid of, we must remove from our surroundings the cues and opportunities (the temptations) that support them.

I suggest you create a list of your habits/addictions. Write down what you perceive to be the most frequent negative things you do. What activities take up most of your time? What do I think about most of the day? Think about the things that have become distractions from God. Note the obvious ones. Discovering the less obvious ones will require time. Ask your spouse, significant other, close friends, and/or family to share their observations. They may not want to hurt your feelings. Tell them you desire an honest answer and won't get upset. Remain calm.

MAKING THE CHANGES

When I quit smoking, every time I desired a cigarette I'd chew on a piece of deliciously sweet *Juicy Fruit* gum. At first it was one piece, but soon I chewed 6 pieces at once to get more and more sweet juiciness. Long story short—I got addicted to *Juicy Fruit*. Scientists have found that sugar is addictive and stimulates the same pleasure centers of the brain as hard-core drugs. Getting off sugar leads to withdrawal and cravings, requiring an actual detox process to wean off. *Here I go again!*

Many professionals suggest changing to a different behavior, as in "behavior modification." The problem is this doesn't allow people to be internally transformed, but rather pushes them to merely conform or become addicted to something else. We can't merely modify our behavior because the underlying issue still exists, and we'll eventually switch to another behavior, like musical chairs.

Many people fear "stopping" their favorite/addictive thing. Don't look at it as "stopping" something; change your mindset to see it as *starting something new and different*—with God.

One thing we should do is *make the decision to deal with the underlying reasons and pain.* Lamentations 3:40 states, *"Instead, let us test and examine our ways. Let us turn back to the LORD."* Most people finally realize that they'll never stay sober until they find out the reason they'd become an alcoholic or people-pleaser or bulimic, for example.

Ask God, "Why the insatiable cravings? What am I trying to cover up?" This is the process of exploring the reasons why we do what we do. (You may need to seek guidance from a professional counselor who can help you break down large barriers. Perhaps one of my other biblical counseling books will help you. See page 173.)

TAKE CONTROL OF YOUR ENVIRONMENT

Our environment is composed of cues that can prompt our behavior and influence is without our even realizing it. *We can decide to take control over our environment.* There is no reason to permit unwanted influences to continue. For example, if you have an extended family photo on your desk at work, and every time you look at it your eyes scan in on your back-stabbing sister-in-law → which triggers you to go to Starbucks and buy a super-sugary latte → remove the picture. If you get triggered on Facebook to feel inferior or "less than," either close your account or choose a new group of friends or choose to take more control over your newsfeeds. *This is removing the cues and opportunities from your environment.*

Hebrews 12:1 states, *"Let us strip off every weight that slows us down, especially the sin that so easily trips us up."* I say *tackle the triggers.* It's important to specifically identify triggers and avoid them. Most often, triggers are situations and/or emotions we're not aware of. Document episodes in order to look for trigger patterns. Ask yourself the *who, what, when, where, how,* and *why* questions:

- When and where are you most tempted?
- How do you usually feel when you're most tempted?
- What happened right before you did this behavior?
- Who is with you when you're tempted …?
- Why do you think this happens?

CREATE A NEW SENSE OF SELF-CONTROL

Research confirms that people with good *self-control* (a fruit of the Spirit) manage their lives better. They create good routine habits which eventually become unconscious.[79] We can carve out areas where we do have control. For example, binge eating is a very common habit and addiction. When craving a particular food, instead of constantly telling yourself "Don't do it'" instead create a situation where you can say yes. Tara, a binge eater, created a chart that had a list of the foods she could eat (wise choices). As she put it, "This eating machine could eat all day as long as the food was on the chart." Tara's solution gave her back a sense of control.

For example, consider developing the habit of encouraging others; of truthfulness; of good temper. The more you practice implementing positive behaviors—which begins with thinking positive thoughts—the more habitual and easier they will become the next time and the next time—until they become second nature.

† *What is God saying to you? What are you going to do about it?*

29 — A BEAUTIFUL MIND

A beautiful mind is ...

What does a "beautiful mind" mean to you? What qualities of your mind would you say you prize the most?

Think of all the changes in your thinking that have taken place since you began the *Turn Your Mind and Brain Back On* study. Perhaps you're disappointed with the pace at which God is transforming you and your mind. Don't be discouraged:

> *But we Christians have no veil over our faces; we can be mirrors that brightly reflect the glory of the Lord. And as the Spirit of the Lord works within us, we become more and more like him (2 Corinthians 3:8).*

You are becoming more like Jesus and thinking with His mind, whether you realize it or not. Throughout the Bible we see the people who were transformed were most often changed slowly, over time. I feel this way a lot, like very little progress is being made day to day. But when I look backwards, I see God has been doing a great work in me. This seems to be the consensus of most mature Christians. Be assured: God is at work in you—gradually reflecting more fully His image.

One Christlike characteristic that God is constantly chipping away in me, and dare I say most other Christians due to our flesh nature, is pride and self-centeredness. It reminds me of this story:

> A well-known Christian businessman was speaking at a church. He got carried away boasting to the congregation about all God had given him: a successful business, a large home, a great family, a famous name, and enough money to travel and give to charities. He commented that many people would love to change places with him. Then he exclaimed, "What more could God give me?"
>
> From the back a voice yelled, "A dose of humility!"

No one wants their pride exposed or to feel humiliated. Humiliation and humility are not the same, although they often feel the same. *Humiliation* is brought upon us by others (including the devil) and often in the presence of others. It cuts deeper than embarrassment and diminishes our pride and dignity.

Contrarily, the Bible describes "humility" as a meekness and absence of self—void of Flesh Woman. It's pulling back the curtain to show others who we really are. Humility is literally translated as "lowliness of mind" which we could translate as "a beautiful mind." God regards it as a very important characteristic. Romans 12:3 puts it, *"Do not think of yourself more highly than you ought, but rather think of yourself with sober judgment* [be honest in your estimate of yourself]. *"*

If you are ever in doubt about what makes a person great, don't look to celebrities or the billionaires of society; look at Jesus. It was He who proclaimed, *"I have washed your feet, you also should wash one another's feet" (John 13:14).* Jesus did not humble Himself in the presence of others because His self-esteem was low. He chose to serve them— wash their feet—because He loved them. Jesus says importance is not found in possessions, power or prestige. It's found in service, character and humility—in Christ.

Just look at what God does when we humble ourselves:

- *James 4:10*: Humble yourselves before the Lord, and **he will lift you up.**
- *Psalm 18:27:* You [God] **rescue** the humble …
- *Psalm 25:9:* He **leads** the humble in doing right, **teaching them** his way.
- *Psalm 147:6:* The LORD **supports** the humble …

BEAUTIFUL MINDS START WITH GRATITUDE

Previously I shared my experience of being a featured speaker on *Focus on the Family Weekend* show (see page 88). The entire experience reminded me of when I turned 8-years-old. For my birthday I asked for a new Barbie doll and the Barbie sports car. For months I envisioned me and Barbie driving everywhere together. The big day came. I couldn't tear the wrapping paper off fast enough. My mind was way ahead.

In a few moments, my hot new Barbie will be driving down the highway of our hallway in her new cool sports car! Where shall we go first, Barbie? Wait a minute … where's the car? All that's in this package is Barbie. I got gypped!

That's how I felt when I listened to the interview and Bill Maier didn't mention my book. After seeing my ATE of pride, I took my feelings to God and confessed I had an ungrateful attitude. Instead of thanking Him for the opportunity to merely share my story and ministry, I turned it into a woe is me moment—a *Where's the car?* moment. Score: Satan!

✝✝✝

The Bible says, *"Be sure to fear the LORD and serve him faithfully with all your heart; consider what great things he has done for you" (1 Samuel 12:24).* In this verse we are told to do three things:

1. *Fear the Lord* (to display a spirit of reverence and respect for God).
2. *Serve Him.*
3. *Acknowledge the great things He has done for you.*

Let's tie this back to Romans 12:2, the focus of this study.

Don't copy the behavior and customs of this world, but let God transform you into a new person by changing the way you think. Then you will learn to know God's will for you, which is good and pleasing and perfect.

Our mind controls our body, but our will controls our mind. God wants us to not only surrender our minds to Him so He may transform them, but also our wills. So, what is God's good and pleasing will? First Samuel 12:24 just told us:

1. *Fear the Lord.*
2. *Serve Him.*
3. *Acknowledge the great things He has done for you.*

That is to say: *We are here to bless and love God*, not the other way around—to use Him like a supermarket genie. Consider the words of the *Shorter Westminster Catechism:* "The chief end of man is to serve God and enjoy him forever." In fact, empirical evidence shows that human beings may be born with a desire for a relationship with a "Transcendent Other," and that longing begins to reveal itself in children as young as 3-years-old.[80]

Unfortunately, the "behaviors and customs of this world" teach us the very opposite. Our society has been in the midst of raising generations of narcissists whose only sense of self is around entitlement and becoming rich and famous. In the first chapter of *A Purpose-Driven Life*, Rick Warren writes,

> It's not about you. The purpose of your life is far greater than your own personal fulfillment, your peace of mind, or even your happiness. It's far greater than your family, your career, or even your wildest dreams and ambitions. If you want to know why you were placed on this planet, you must begin with God. You were born *by* his purpose and *for* his purpose.[81]

We've done some great life work with God in transforming our beliefs and thoughts. When God calls us to self-examination it is because He loves us and desires to transform us into more mature Christ-like children. Now, consider what you were created for:

- *Love and know intimately the only true God and His Son, Jesus Christ*, finding life in that knowledge by developing a compassionate relationship with God. The psalmist said, *"It is good for me to draw near to God"* *(Psalm 73:28, KJV)*.

- *Enjoy healthy relationships in an intimate environment.* As a society we have become withdrawn which is detrimental to our personal and spiritual growth. It is in relating to others we grow the most. When we find a person or group committed to authentic relationships, we find God and something very beautiful. Ecclesiastes 4:11-12 states,

  "On a cold night, two under the same blanket gain warmth from each other, but how can one be warm alone? And one standing alone can be attacked and defeated, but two can stand back-to-back and conquer; three is even better, for a triple-braided cord is not easily broken."

- *Leave our mark on the world.* First Corinthians 12:7 says, *"Each person is given something to do that shows who God is"* (MSG). Our greatest mark is to love others and be Christlike to every person we come in contact with. (Read Matthew 25: 31-46.)

Our purpose is not to copy or out do the next person or to become famous and accumulate wealth. Every person—which includes you— has been set apart to do something no one else can do. God tells us, *"Before I formed you in the womb I knew you, before you were born I set you apart"* (Jeremiah 1:5). We all ask, "What am I here for? What is my destiny?" Only time with God will answer that.

We spent time learning about our conflict zones because the days ahead will be filled with opportunities and temptations intended to entice us to invest our time and energy away from God. *Invest your life and time wisely.* I don't know about you, but when I'm united with Jesus in heaven I want to hear Him say to me His words in Matthew 25:23, *"Well done good and faithful servant."*

Barry Manilow's classic song, *Just One Voice*, says it well,

Just one voice, singing in the darkness, all it takes is one voice, singing so they hear what's on your mind, and when you look around you'll find there's more than one voice, singing in the darkness, joining with your one voice … hands are joined and fears unlocked, if only one voice would start it on its own, we need just one voice facing the unknown, and everyone will sing!

30 — The Power of Thankfulness

When you wake up in the morning, do you say, "Good morning, Lord 😊" or, "Good Lord, it's morning 😞" Pessimism and ingratitude is certainly a present-day problem.

There are lots of scientific studies bearing that thankfulness and gratitude as an essential component of health, wholeness and well-being. The prize: a better functioning brain and heart and the peace of God. It's a fact: People who approach life with an "attitude of gratitude" are generally healthier, happier and not depressed. It is now one of the treatment modalities for people with depression. It's harder for seeds of depression to take root in a grateful heart.

No wonder the Bible has long embraced gratitude as an indispensable virtue. What about when things don't turn out, like disasters, accidents, abuse, job losses or cancer? The Bible instructs us to *"give thanks in all circumstances, for this is God's will for you in Christ Jesus" (1 Thessalonians 5:18)*. Notice the verse does not say to give thanks *for* all circumstances, but to give thanks *in* all circumstances. There's a big difference.

We know God is not the author of evil and tragedy. Man makes bad choices and Satan is doing his evil thing 24/7. God's ways are mysterious and He may allow bad stuff to happen, but we have the assurance that in the midst of a trying situation, He is working in it. Nothing, even though it may have the earmarks of Satan all over it, can separate us from His love and mercy (Romans 8:38-39). *His provision empowers us against all enemies.* Believing this can create a grateful and beautiful mind and heart. *I will praise you God despite this bad situation!*

Being thankful in a dire circumstance can only be done by faith. It goes against Flesh Woman's nature. We can choose to pray, *Father, I'm in a bad place right now. I don't want to be here, but You, in your love and wisdom allowed it for me. I thank You for what You're about to do.*

God works by paradox. We accept God's perfect provision of grace and power because His power is made perfect in our weakness (2 Corinthians 12:9).

Luke tells the story about ten lepers who asked Jesus for healing. They were all cleansed. *"One of them, when he saw he was healed, came back, praising God in a loud voice" (Luke 17:15).* Only *one* of the 10 lepers came back. The returning leper didn't thank God so he could get more. He just thanked God. Deuteronomy 6:4 tells us to love God with *all* of our hearts and minds. This means we shouldn't merely love God with the part of our heart and mind that is happy, but with the angry and sad part too.

- *Always give thanks for everything to our God and Father in the name of our Lord Jesus Christ (Ephesians 5:20).*
- *... and come with him into the presence of God the Father to give him your thanks (Colossians 3:17).*

Maya Angelou said, "Let gratitude be the pillow upon which you kneel to say your nightly prayer." Although past pain cannot be forgotten, it can be rewritten by new experiences that are positive and transformative. Invest in focusing on *at least* one blessing per day. I challenge you to change the cycle of thinking from: "What more do I need?" to "Thank you Lord for what I have."

BLESSING GOD

Humility—Gratefulness—Thankfulness—what we're talking about here is an attitudinal lifestyle change; redirecting our aim. Jesus had a formula to make His points: "You have heard that it was said ... But I tell you ..." Jesus expects us to "go beyond the minimum."

When the Jewish people pray, *"Bless the LORD, O my soul, And all that is within me, bless His holy name" (Psalm 103:1, NASB)*— they acknowledge Him as the source of all blessings. To bless God is to "praise" Him and give thanks for what He's done in your life, and to go beyond the minimum, called worship. We can make it a habit of blessing God with thankfulness and asking, "What more can I do to please you?" Here are some suggestions:

1—EVERYDAY TELL GOD THREE OR MORE THINGS YOU ARE THANKFUL FOR.

As hard as this may be in tough times, we can choose to focus on what we have. This woman was renowned for her cheerful endurance while going through a painful trial of chemotherapy.

> A woman woke up one morning, looked in the mirror and noticed she had only three hairs left on her head. She thought *I'll braid my hair today.* So, she did. She had a wonderful day. The next morning she looked in the mirror and had only two hairs on her head. *Hmm,* she thought. *I'll part my hair down the middle today.* She had a super day. The following day she noticed only one hair left on her head. She thought, *What can I do with one hair? A ponytail!* She had a really fun day. The following day she noticed there wasn't a single hair on her head. "Yay!" she exclaimed. "I don't have to fix my hair today!" She had a fabulous day.

We *always* have at least one thing to be thankful for—even if it's only one hair. Embrace God's little blessings: the air you breathe, your family, reliable transportation, groceries, hot water to shower with, a reliable friend. Through this study, no doubt, God has brought hope and healing into your life and demolished some big strongholds. Praise Him for that. When was the last time you thanked God for your salvation and for delivering you from the world's bondage, or thanked him for your health, intellect, talents and gifts, or that His love and mercy have covered your past?

2—WRITE A GRATITUDE LETTER.

Tell some people in your life (like a relative, friend, or a person that influenced you) what it is about them you are thankful for. Not only will your life be more joyful—so will theirs!

3—PAY IT FORWARD.

Secretly do something nice for someone. This is Christ in action. We may also find it has a boomerang effect: we send it out to someone and they return a kind act.

✝ *What is a daily and weekly habit you can commit to that will help you appreciate God's goodness and grace, and motivate you to do something new to please Him?*

You're Done!

Congratulations on completing this study! This is quite an accomplishment. There's an excitement in heaven I believe. Like Paul, you can now say, *"I have fought the good fight, I have finished the race, I have kept the faith" (2 Timothy 4:7).* It's been rough, but your courage and faith in God got you through. You have the power to be a history maker; to write your own legacy.

Many ask, "When does mind renewal end?" The answer is never. As broken, fallible humans living in a shattered world, the process of working towards thinking like Jesus really never ends. But the power of old toxic thinking patterns undeniably diminishes with time.

Our stories have changed; our identities have changed; our lives have changed. There has been transformation! Take the time to delight in your growth, your new relationship in Christ and your success. *Celebrate who you are now*—a beautiful, spiritually healthy, delightful, joyous child of God; no longer shackled by the need to be better, perfect or something you're not. God bless you!

Follow the path of the unsafe, independent thinker. Expose your ideas to the dangers of controversy. Speak your mind and fear less the label of 'crackpot' than the stigma of conformity. And on issues that seem important to you, stand up and be counted at any cost.

—Puritan preacher Thomas J. Watson

ABOUT THE AUTHOR

 **K**imberly Davidson lived two decades of her life in complete turmoil; in pain and addiction. Jesus heard the cry of her heart. He saw her pain and interceded, freeing her in 1989 from her personal prison. Today she uses her pen to write curriculum and books for women in pain—writing her legacy.

As a board-certified pastoral counselor, Kimberly helps women mend their souls. She received her MA in specialized ministry from Western Seminary, Portland, Oregon; a BA in health sciences from the University of Iowa. She considers herself a lifelong learner. Kimberly has ministered to women for over 15-years, from within prison walls to youth centers, inspiring others to empower God to meet their emotional and spiritual needs.

She created *Olive Branch Outreach*, an interactive website dedicated to bring hope and restoration to those struggling with body image, abuse and food addiction. In addition, Kimberly leads an abuse recovery program at a federal women's prison. She is also the director of education for *Freedom Calling*, a ministry dedicated to the education and prevention of sex trafficking; and is a contributor to *Living in Truth*, a ministry that helps women who struggle with unhealthy eating and body image.

Kimberly has authored or contributed to 17 books. She lives in Oregon on a small ranch with her husband and critters.

Connect with Kimberly

If you want to connect with Kimberly, you can through her website at *OliveBranchOutreach.com* or on *Facebook*. Or, email her at *kim@kimdavidson.com*. She'd love to hear from you or meet you at a future event.

Other Books by Kimberly Davidson

I'm Beautiful? Why Can't I See It? [2nd Edition]
Love Yourself and Love Your Body in 12 Weeks

Eyes Wide Open
Love Yourself and Love Your Body in 12 Weeks
This is a 9-week version of *I'm Beautiful? Why Can't I See It?*

I'm God's Girl? Why Can't I Feel It?
Daily Biblical Encouragement to Defeat Depression & the Blues

The Perfect Counselor
Break Through Your Past to Ensure a Healthy Future

Dancing In the Sonshine (Second Edition)
Restoration from the Wounds of Abuse
(Some chapters in The Perfect Counselor are also in Dancing in the Sonshine)

Something Happened On My Way to Hell
Break Free from the Insatiable Pursuit of Pleasure

Breaking the Cover Girl Mask: *Toss Out Toxic Thoughts*

Deadly Love: *Confronting the Sex Trafficking of Our Children*

Foundations
Empowering Youth to Establish Healthy Sexuality & Relationships
(A Parent's and Youth Leader's Guide)

Torn Between Two Masters
Encouraging Teens to Live Authentically in a Celebrity-Obsessed World

REFERENCES

[1] John Bargh, PhD, *Before You Know It* (NY: Touchstone, 2018), 250.

[2] Bond and DePaulo, *Personality and Social Psychology Review,* Accuracy of deception judgments (2006), pp. 214-34.

[3] John Bargh, PhD, *Before You Know It* (NY: Touchstone, 2018), 184.

[4] Anne Moir, *Brain Sex: The Real Difference Between Men and Women,* 33-37, New York: Dell Publishing, 1991.

[5] Wikipedia: http://en.wikipedia.org/wiki/Mind.

[6] Ai AL, Peterson C, Tice TN, H.B. Rodgers, Bolling SF: The influence of prayer coping on mental health among cardiac patients; J Health Psychol. 2007 Jul; 12(4), 580-96.

[7] Caroline Leaf, "How Prayer Affects the Brain: Prayer and Healing."

[8] Joseph Murphy, *The Power of Your Subconscious Mind,* 1963.

[9] Paraphrase from an anonymous email forward chain.

[10] Caroline Leaf, *Who Switched Off My Brain,* 4, 8, 125, Switch On Your Brain Organisation Pty (Ltd.), 2007

[11] Ibid.

[12] Ibid, 8, 113-114, 94.

[13] Source: Dr. Caroline Leaf; TBN, May 25, 2016

[14] Caroline Leaf, *Who Switched Off My Brain,* 113-114, Switch On Your Brain Organisation Pty (Ltd.), 2007.

[15] Drs. Michael A. & William Mitchell, "Habits—They Can Make or Break Your Child," *ParentLife,* March 1998, p. 6.

[16] Charles Duhigg, *The Power of Habit* (NY: Random House, 2014), xvi.

[17] Norman Doidge, *The Brain that Changes Itself,* (New York: Penguin Books, 2007), 114-115.

[18] Ibid, 20.

[19] Fredrike Bannink, *Post Traumatic Success* (W.W. Norton & Company, 2014) 174.

[20] See: http://www.nytimes.com/2012/03/24/your-money/why-people-remember-negative-events-more-than-positive-ones.html?_r=0.

[21] Gillath, Shaver, Wendleken, Mikulincer, "Attachment-style differences in the ability to suppress negative thoughts," *Neurimage.* 2005 Dec; 28 (4): 835-47

[22] www.westernseminary.edu/files/publications/magazine/WS_Magazine_Fall2016.

[23] See: http://www.nytimes.com/2012/03/24/your-money/why-people-remember-negative-events-more-than-positive-ones.html?_r=0.

[24] Stated by Drs. Timothy Jennings and Caroline Leaf.

[25] Source: Dr. Caroline Leaf; TBN, "The Disordered Mind;" March 9, 2016.

[26] Linda Graham, *Bouncing Back* (Novato: New World Library, 2013), 11-13.

[27] Caroline Leaf, "How Prayer Affects the Brain: Prayer and Healing."

[28] Charles Duhigg, *The Power of Habit* (NY: Random House, 2014), xiv-xv.

[29] Carrington Steele, *Don't Drink the Kool-Aid,*1, © 2008 Carrington Steele

[30] Archibald Hart, "Lovers of Pleasures," *Christian Counseling Today,* 13, Vol. 16 No. 2, 2009.

[31] CNN.com, *Mother Teresa's Letters Reveal Doubts*, September 7, 2001, accessed February 16, 2008.

[32] Daniel G. Amen, M.D. *Making a Good Brain Great,* 152, New York: Three Rivers Press, 2005.

[33] Robert J. Morgan, *Then Sings My Soul* (Nashville: Thomas Nelson, 2011) 157.

[34] Joe Navarro, *What Every Body is Saying* (NY: HarperCollins, 2008) 29, 206-207.

[35] Louie Giglio, Excerpted from "Examining My Past for a Better Future I-II" on the *Focus on the Family* daily radio broadcast #1002630; 2014.

[36] Archibald Hart, "Lovers of Pleasures," *Christian Counseling Today,* 13, Vol. 16 No. 2, 2009.

[37] Pete A. Sanders, Jr., *Access Your Brain's Joy Center: The Free Soul Method,* 3, Sedona: Free Soul, 1996.

[38] Timothy Jennings, *The God Shaped Brain* (Downers Grove: IVP Books, 2013).

[39] John Bargh, PhD, *Before You Know It* (NY: Touchstone, 2018), 217.

[40] Charles Haddon Spurgeon, *Spurgeon's Sermons, Vol. 1,* 126-127, Grand Rapids: Baker Book House, 1983.

[41] Cheryl Forbes, *Imagination,* Quoted in: David Needham, *Birthright: Christian, Do You Know Who You Are?,* 184-185, Sisters: Multonomah Publishers, 1999.

[42] Tim Hartford, "How to Save Smarter," *Parade,* 10, May 10, 2009.

[43] Dwight L. Moody Quotes:

http://thinkexist.com/quotes/dwight_l._moody/3.html; accessed June 2, 2008.

[44] John Bargh, PhD, *Before You Know It* (NY: Touchstone, 2018), 205-207.

[45] Ibid.

[46] Quoted by: Drew Pinsky and S. Mark Young, *The Mirror Effect,* (New York: HarperCollins, 2009), 139

[47] *Fox News,* October 27, 2010;

http://www.foxnews.com/entertainment/2010/10/27/charlie-sheens-career-remains-solid-amid-personal-issues-experts-say

[48] http://www.theology.ie/thinkers/girard.htm

[49] David Jeremiah, *Turning Points,* September 4, 2008.

[50] Bob Sorge, *Dealing with the Rejection and Praise of Man,* "Rejection: God's Specialty" (Greenwood: Oasis House, 2002).

[51] Ibid, 40.

[52] Ibid, 85.

[53] Ibid, November 14, 2008.

[54] http://www.transcendyourlimits.com/fear-is-not-real-after-earth.

[55] Newberg and Waldman, *How God Changes Your Brain,* 39.

[56] A. Newberg, MD & M. R. Walman, *How God Changes Your Brain* (New York: Ballantine Books, 2010), 132.

[57] Fredrike Bannink, *Post Traumatic Success* (W.W. Norton & Company, 2014) 175.

[58] Brene Brown, *Daring Greatly* (New York: Gotham Books, 2012) 67.

[59] Brené Brown, *Rising Strong* (New York: Random House, 2017), 276.

[60] Simon Baron-Cohen, *The Science of Evil* (New York: Basic Books, 2011) 6-11.

[61] Ibid, 6-20.

[62] David W. Jones, *The Psychology of Jesus,* 2014; 110.

[63] Bob Sorge, *Dealing with the Rejection and Praise of Man,* "Your Source of Acceptance" (Greenwood: Oasis House, 2002).

[64] Joshua Ryan Butler, *The Skeletons in God's Closet* (Nashville: W Publishing Group, 2104), 261.

[65] G. Jantz, *Hope, Help, and Healing for Eating Disorders* (Wheaton: Harold Shaw 1995), 125.

[66] See Leviticus 19:18; Deuteronomy 32:35; Proverbs 24:12; Romans 12:17-21; 1 Thessalonians 5:15; Hebrews 10:30.

[67] Brene Brown, *Rising Strong* (New York: Random House, 2017), 115.

[68] Used by Permission: *The Voice of the Martyrs,* htttp://www.persecution.com.

[69] Neil T. Anderson, *The Bondage Breaker,* (Eugene: Harvest House, 2000, 2nd Rev.), 69, 72.

[70] Cecil Osborne, *The Art of Understanding Yourself* (Grand Rapids: Zondervan, 1982), 87.

[71] Caroline Leaf, *The Perfect You* (Grand Rapids: Baker Books, 2017) 90.

[72] Norman Doidge, "On Neuroplasticity."

[73] Lisa M. Najavits, *Seeking Safety* (The Guilford Press, 2002), 289.

[74] John M. Gottman, *The Seven Principles for Making Marriage Work.*

[75] John Bargh, PhD, *Before You Know It* (NY: Touchstone, 2018), 278.

[76] Ibid.

[77] Arlene Drake, *Carefontation* (New York: Regan Arts., 2017), 17-18.

[78] Marc Lewis, PhD, *The Biology of Desire* (New York: Public Affairs, 2015).

[79] John Bargh, PhD, *Before You Know It* (NY: Touchstone, 2018), 276.

[80] See Justin Barrett, *Why Would Anyone Believe in God?* (Walnut Creek: Altamira Press, 2004).

[81] Rick Warren, *The Purpose Driven Life,* (Grand Rapids, Zondervan, 2002), 17

88413787R00102

Made in the USA
San Bernardino, CA
12 September 2018